"An invaluable resource that offers a fresh perspective, packed with practical insights for embedding learning science within all aspects of talent management."

Tal Goldhamer, *Chief Learning Officer, International Professional services firm*

"Talent Management is crucial, yet often misunderstood without the science. *Uniting Learning Science and Talent Management: Org Scholars'* scientific insights on talent acquisition, employee development, and succession planning are powerful and will truly help organizations advance. It's a practical resource. I highly recommend this book!"

Netta Jenkins, *CEO, Aerodei*

"A research-backed toolkit that connects theory into real situations, with rich examples that will help you improve every dimension of how you grow and manage your people, and therefore your business."

Pep Carrera, *Multi-time CEO*

"*Uniting Learning Science and Talent Management* begs to be read. By fusing the fields of organizational development and learning science, Nebel and Damani offer a fresh perspective that is equal parts usable and discerning. This book is a must-read for anyone seeking to improve their approach to talent management."

Dr. Matthew Campbell, *Senior Lecturer, Vanderbilt University, USA*

"Cindy and Zohra 'walk the talk' in their approach to uniting learning science and talent management by applying insights from the former to ongoing challenges of the latter. Their coverage is practical and comprehensive, making this is a must read for professionals in the Talent Management field."

Dr. Jeanie M. Forray, *Seneca Consortium LLC*

Uniting Learning Science and Talent Management

This book delves into the intricate relationship between the talent lifecycle and learning science, offering a fresh perspective on talent management. Through a meticulous exploration of talent acquisition, management, retention, and exits, it reveals how learning science can be harnessed to enhance organizational growth and employee satisfaction.

Covering strategic talent sourcing, optimized onboarding, leadership development, and innovative retention strategies, the book presents evidence-based approaches to navigating the complexities of the talent cycle. It underscores the transformative power of learning science in creating sustainable talent experiences, processes, programs, and systems. Through real-world applications and theoretical insights, readers gain access to practical strategies for unlocking the true potential within organizations, making it an indispensable resource for talent leaders and HR professionals.

Targeted at HR professionals, talent leaders, organizational developers, and academic researchers, this book serves as a comprehensive guide for those committed to fostering a culture of continuous learning and growth within their organizations. Its practical insights and evidence-based strategies are particularly valuable for professionals seeking to apply learning science principles to real-world challenges in the talent cycle.

Cynthia Nebel is the Director of Learning Services at St. Louis University School of Medicine and resides in Cottleville, MO, USA.

Zohra (Zo) Damani is a seasoned talent development professional and an acclaimed author, currently serving as a Training Specialist at Starbucks Reserve in Seattle, USA.

Uniting Learning Science and Talent Management

Org Scholars

Cynthia Nebel and Zohra Damani

Routledge
Taylor & Francis Group

NEW YORK AND LONDON

Cover Image: urfinguss via Getty Images

First published 2025
by Routledge
605 Third Avenue, New York, NY 10158

and by Routledge
4 Park Square, Milton Park, Abingdon, Oxon OX14 4RN

Routledge is an imprint of the Taylor & Francis Group, an informa business

Library of Congress Cataloging-in-Publication Data
Names: Nebel, Cynthia, author. | Damani, Zohra, author.
Title: Uniting learning science and talent management : org scholars / Cynthia Nebel and Zohra Damani.
Description: New York, NY : Routledge, 2025. | Includes bibliographical references and index.
Identifiers: LCCN 2024021373 (print) | LCCN 2024021374 (ebook) | ISBN 9781032711584 (hardback) | ISBN 9781032711560 (paperback) | ISBN 9781032711591 (ebook)
Subjects: LCSH: Personnel management. | Manpower planning. | Organizational effectiveness. | Organizational learning.
Classification: LCC HF5549 .N356 2025 (print) | LCC HF5549 (ebook) | DDC 658.3—dc23/eng/20240620
LC record available at https://lccn.loc.gov/2024021373
LC ebook record available at https://lccn.loc.gov/2024021374

ISBN: 978-1-032-71158-4 (hbk)
ISBN: 978-1-032-71156-0 (pbk)
ISBN: 978-1-032-71159-1 (ebk)

DOI: 10.4324/9781032711591

Typeset in Optima
by Apex CoVantage, LLC

Contents

About the Authors

Dr. Cynthia Nebel is the Director of Learning Services at St. Louis University School of Medicine. She earned her Ph.D. in the Brain, Behavior, and Cognition program at Washington University in St. Louis and has served as Assistant Chair of Psychology at Lindenwood University, Associate Professor of Psychology at Washburn University, and Senior Lecturer in the Leadership and Learning in Organizations doctorate program at Vanderbilt University. Dr. Nebel has broad interests in human learning and memory and applying the science of learning to educational contexts. She has presented keynotes and workshops at regional and national conferences in the US, as well as abroad at many schools and conferences of educators in the UK and Australia, and government and Fortune 500 corporate organizations. She has also consulted for a number of ed tech companies and educational institutions. Dr. Nebel is passionate about bridging the gap between research and practice in education and serves as an active collaborator of the Learning Scientists (www.learningscientists.org). Together with the Learning Scientists, she co-authored *Ace That Test: A Student's Guide to Learning Better.*

Zohra (Zo) Damani stands at the confluence of transformative thought, action, and holistic well-being, weaving her expertise as a visionary author and a distinguished talent development professional across various industries. Her career has been deeply rooted in people, culture, and development, where her contributions have significantly shaped the ethos and dynamics of various sectors including consulting, technology, ed tech, law firms, manufacturing, and nonprofit organizations. Her forthcoming role in the food and beverage industry as a training specialist marks a strategic pivot, allowing her to infuse her doctoral learnings into the fabric of this new domain, showcasing her versatility and commitment to applying academic insights in practical scenarios. Her academic pursuit, a Doctorate of Education (Ed.D.) with a focus on learning and leadership at Vanderbilt, culminating in summer 2024, underscores her unwavering commitment to fostering transformative changes within the talent cycle. Her global thought leadership is highlighted by her presentations at prestigious platforms such as the National Science Academy of Uganda, where she has spoken on bridging the DEI gap, showcasing her commitment to fostering inclusivity and understanding across diverse cultural contexts. Zohra's commitment to personal and professional growth is further enriched by certifications in life coaching and yoga training, alongside her pursuit of shamanic practitioner training in Scotland. These pursuits embody the spirit of a lifelong learner and leader, dedicated to advancing talent development and organizational growth through her innovative writing, professional engagements, academic research, and spiritual practices. Her journey is a testament to the synergy of intellectual depth, professional versatility, and holistic wellness, poised to make a lasting impact in the realms of talent management and beyond.

Acknowledgements

Above all, we want to thank God, the universe, or whatever divine force brought us together to make this project happen. We want to thank our colleagues, friends, and peers in the Vanderbilt LLO program for creating the kind of environment that allows for interdisciplinary dialogue and innovation. Without the hard work and dedication of the faculty and students in that program, this project would not exist. We would also like to thank the editorial team at Routledge for their support (Zoe Thomson and Maddie Gray) and the reviewers for their useful feedback.

Cindy would like to thank Dr. Rob Tigner for lighting the fire for her passion for learning and the Learning Scientists for giving her the platform to develop as a science communicator and for their constant and unwavering support. The community of passionate, strong women we've developed has shaped so much of my academic identity. Huge thanks to Jamie Bolar for picking up the slack when needed and cheering me on, and all of my colleagues at SLU who have been so supportive. I would also like to thank my dearest friends, Emily, Stefanie, and Mary Jo, and my parents, Jayne and Ed, for their constant source of love in all of life's phases. And more than anyone I thank my family for being my inspiration and my joy. Thank you Steve for staying by my side through all the ups and downs; Lindsey for never letting me overthink the good things in life; Teddy, for helping me see the world for all its beauty and wonder, and especially Annabelle for singing us through our meetings and being the sunshine on all the cloudy days. Finally, thanks to Zo for spinning all my crazy ideas into something we could both be proud of. Thanks for following the signs with me!

Zohra (Zo) begins with a heartfelt expression of gratitude to the divine force that guided us through this journey. This book, a harmonious fusion of disparate realms into a single, unified vision, stands as a testament to the divine inspiration that fuels our creative and intellectual pursuits. It's a celebration of divine synchronicity, where ideas and insights transcend the ordinary, weaving together the threads of knowledge and wisdom. To her beloved parents (Jeff and Rose), whose souls now rest in the serenity of peace, she owes the foundation of this endeavor. Their decision to bring Zo to the United States was driven by a singular pursuit of higher education, a legacy that this book proudly carries forward. Their dreams, aspirations, and sacrifices are the invisible ink on these pages, a silent yet profound presence that continues to guide and inspire. Zo's gratitude extends to her brother (Jalal Damani), sister-in-law (Nirmeen Rajani), and nephews (Kalel and Krish), whose unwavering support and belief have been the beacon of hope in moments of doubt and despair. Their love, encouragement, and the light they bring into her life push her to continue on this path, even when the journey seems impossible.

Last, she extends her deepest thanks to Cindy Nebel, whose late-night email after class sparked the inception of this book. Cindy's suggestion was not just a moment of academic insight; it was the catalyst that transformed a fleeting thought into a tangible reality. Her belief in the potential of our combined efforts to create something meaningful, her encouragement, and her intellectual companionship throughout this process have been invaluable. This book, a culmination of divine inspiration, familial legacy, unwavering support, and collaborative spirit, is a tribute to all who have been a part of this journey (endorsers, publisher, reviewers, friends). It's a reminder that the most profound achievements are often the result of collective endeavor, guided by a higher power and rooted in love and support. To all who have contributed to this journey, Zo's gratitude knows no bounds.

1 Purpose of This Book: The Why

Figure 1.1 iStock.com/Yutthana Gaetgeaw

Source: https://www.istockphoto.com/faq/using-files#illustrations-and-vectors

Welcome to a journey that navigates the intriguing intersection of learning science and talent management. This book is a collaborative endeavor by Cindy, a cognitive psychologist, and Zohra, a seasoned professional in the corporate world. This story starts at Vanderbilt University, where Zohra was completing her doctorate and Cindy was teaching a course on learning science. On that fateful evening, Zohra made a comment in class that was *profound*. The class was stunned into silence. And then . . . we all

DOI: 10.4324/9781032711591-1

signed off for the evening and the moment was gone. But Cindy noticed the weight of that moment and emailed Zohra at 10pm on a random Wednesday night to tell her that she needed to write that book, to get that idea out there. And she responded, "How about *we* write this book"? And here we are, embarking on an adventure to merge academia and practical wisdom into a compelling narrative that challenges conventions and sparks innovation.

Cindy brings her academic expertise in understanding how individuals learn and retain information, delving into cognitive psychology. Her academic journey has been focused on optimizing these learning processes and her professional life has been spent sharing these processes with stakeholders in every level of education, government, and corporate organizations. Zohra, in contrast, brings a wealth of practical experience from her extensive career spanning various sectors such as consulting, technology, education technology, and nonprofit organizations. Her expertise lies in the comprehensive spectrum of the talent cycle, encompassing talent acquisition, management, retention, and succession planning, as well as organizational design in environments ranging from startups to large corporations.

In spite of the rich potential of learning theory from cognitive psychology, its practical application in organizational and workforce development has been underutilized. This book aims to bridge this gap, melding these two seemingly disparate fields with a particular focus on the talent cycle. We explore how principles of cognitive psychology, which have proved transformative in academic settings, can similarly revolutionize the workplace. By bringing these two distinct concepts together, the book offers a journey of discovery and insight. It is designed to challenge preconceived notions and invite readers to engage with fresh perspectives, making it a valuable resource for leaders who embrace continuous learning and innovation.

Filling the Gap in Talent Cycle Practices

We have identified significant gaps in current talent cycle practices where the principles of learning science can offer substantial improvements. Challenges such as employee retention and leadership development are areas ripe for the integration of insights from cognitive psychology. Our intention is not to replace organizational theory but to enrich it, applying these evidence-based ideas from learning science to enhance various stages of the talent cycle.

It is crucial to emphasize that this book doesn't aim to comprehensively cover the talent cycle. Instead, it firmly grounds itself in learning science, focusing on how cognitive principles such as memory recall and attention can be effectively harnessed in a corporate setting. While delving into the practical application of these cognitive insights, readers may feel compelled to explore the talent cycle in greater depth. Our primary objective is to furnish readers with an understanding of how learning science can revolutionize and optimize various stages of the talent cycle, ranging from talent acquisition to talent exits.

Join us on this enlightening journey where the realms of cognitive psychology and corporate talent management intersect. This book caters to individuals keen on grasping and implementing the principles of learning science to redefine and elevate the talent cycle within their organizations. Through this exploration, we endeavor to present innovative perspectives and strategies, illuminating the path toward a more efficient and enlightened approach to talent management.

How to Use This Book

Welcome to a resource crafted to serve as a practical guide through the intricate pathways of the talent cycle, enriched with the insights of learning science. Understanding the varied needs of professionals at different stages of their career, this book has been structured to reflect the diverse aspects of the talent cycle. Each chapter is a deep dive into a specific phase, offering targeted insights and strategies.

We recognize that your professional focus and challenges might vary greatly. Therefore, we have designed this book to accommodate a flexible reading approach. You are not bound to read it cover to cover; instead, feel free to navigate directly to the chapter that resonates most with your current needs. Whether your immediate focus lies in tackling talent acquisition hurdles, enhancing employee development programs, or refining succession planning strategies, you will find a dedicated chapter that addresses these specific areas.

Each chapter in this book is designed to be self-contained. This means that you can dive into any chapter and find all the necessary background information, key concepts, and practical applications relevant to that specific aspect of the talent cycle. This structure ensures that even if you choose to read a chapter in isolation, you will gain a comprehensive understanding of the topic at hand.

To further enhance the utility of this book, we have ensured that every chapter strikes a balance between theoretical insights from learning science and their practical application in the corporate world. Real-world examples, case studies, and actionable strategies are interspersed throughout, providing a rich learning experience that is both informative and applicable.

Structured Chapter Layout

Within each chapter, we delve into three core areas:

- **Identifying Challenges:** We begin by outlining common problems specific to that stage of the talent cycle. This real-world contextualization helps in recognizing and understanding the issues at hand.
- **Integrating Learning Science:** Next, we introduce relevant principles of learning science. This section bridges theoretical concepts with practical aspects, offering a deeper understanding of the cognitive processes at play.
- **Practical Application:** The final section of each chapter focuses on applying these scientific principles to real workplace situations. Here, you'll find actionable strategies, case studies, and examples that demonstrate how learning science can resolve specific talent cycle challenges.

This book stands as a beacon for those navigating the complex landscapes of human resources, team leadership, and organizational development. It is not merely a repository of information; it is a compass guiding you towards innovative exploration and practical application. Whether you are an HR professional striving to enhance your organization's talent cycle, a team leader seeking to empower and inspire, or someone deeply involved in shaping the future of organizational development, this book is crafted for you. Its purpose extends beyond providing knowledge—it is designed to equip you with the essential tools and insights necessary to apply learning science effectively, transforming every facet of the talent cycle within your organization.

Return to it as your trusted resource, time and again, to spark exploration and drive meaningful change.

Science of Learning

Throughout this book, you will be introduced to many learning science concepts. But where do these concepts come from and why are we choosing to talk about *these* concepts and not others?

Cognitive psychologists (not to be confused with clinical psychologists) have been studying how people learn for over 100 years.[1] Much of this work has been done in a laboratory setting, not with beakers and chemicals, but with paper and pencil or computers. In the laboratory, psychologists control how long someone spends reading or listening or otherwise learning new content, what they do after learning, and the context in which they try to remember what they learned. Because psychologists

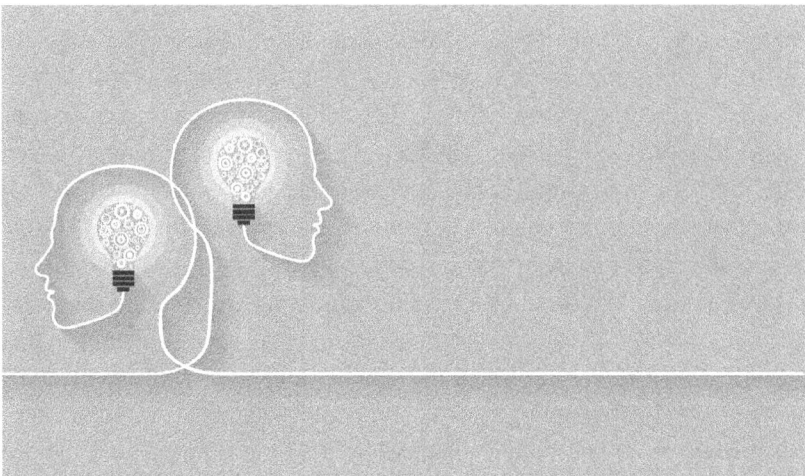

Figure 1.2 iStock.com/Feodora Chiosea
Source: https://www.istockphoto.com/faq/using-files#illustrations-and-vectors

can control so much of the laboratory environment, they are able to conduct experiments in which small changes can be examined to see their effect on learning and memory. Typically, these experiments start with very basic materials. Participants study nonsense syllables,[2] word lists,[3] or paired associates[4] so that researchers can objectively measure how many items they remember.

From these basic laboratory experiments, cognitive psychologists have learned a great deal about the basic processes of memory, attention, and perception. As an example, we have learned that we have two separate memory systems: working memory and long-term memory. Working memory is a limited-capacity system and information must be processed there before it can be moved to long-term storage. Because of this, we cannot attend to everything in our environments and we can really only do one thing at a time.[5] Our knowledge of working memory has huge implications for the learning environments we create for employees and ourselves. In the context of talent development, understanding these cognitive processes is crucial for designing effective training programs and fostering a culture of continuous learning.

But how do we go from very simple laboratory experiments to an understanding of a complex environment like the workplace? After all, in the workplace, time on task is rarely controlled and it is also relatively rare to find people whose roles require a single streamlined task. Cognitive psychologists do not *only* use laboratory research. Once basic processes are understood, cognitive psychologists move to applied laboratory research. In this work, there is still some control, but what individuals are studying now looks a bit more like what they might see in the real world. They might watch a Ted talk,[6] read a passage,[7] or engage in conversation.[8] In this way, psychologists can still examine changes in memory, but in a way that more closely mimics the type of learning that individuals are doing in the real world.

Once researchers have a sense of how learning works with real-world materials, they are ready to examine learning in applied settings. This applied research involves going into environments in which individuals are learning and examining how different contexts impact memory. Often this is done in a classroom setting, where learning is formal and can be assessed on quizzes and tests.[9] It is much more difficult to assess how much learning has taken place in a workplace setting where both learning and recall happens informally, through meetings and conversations.

However, this is where the talent development aspect comes into play, as it's critical to understand how informal learning processes can be harnessed to enhance employee skills and capabilities.

Sometimes, what works in the laboratory is very different when you get to the real world. If folks are having conversations about a meeting topic or needing to apply it to a project they are working on, they might be engaging with that material in a way we don't normally control in the laboratory. Researchers learn something from this applied research and are then able to take research back to the applied laboratory or basic laboratory to examine those factors more closely. This back-and-forth between theory and practice is vital in shaping effective talent development strategies.

Across basic laboratory, applied laboratory, and applied setting research, several specific learning strategies have shown time and time again to improve the retention of information over time. These strategies work in a variety of settings,[10,11] with different types of learners[12,13] and therefore their use can be recommended with a high degree of confidence. For example, if a particular strategy helped medical doctors retain content that they learned in a continuing professional development session, we can be relatively confident that the same strategy would help individuals learn different content while watching a keynote at a conference or listening to a presentation at a weekly meeting. Even though the content differs, the situation is very similar.

Throughout this book, we will be providing ideas for how to improve learning within your organization using strategies that have been tested in many different situations and have decades (or more) of research supporting their use. That is, we will only provide recommendations for strategies that have been vetted through considerable research at all levels. If you see it here, you can be assured that the strategy works in a wide variety of situations and should be particularly effective in talent development, enhancing the skills and knowledge of your workforce.

Applications of Learning Science

So why hasn't this book been written before? If we know so much about how people learn and we've known it for so long, why hasn't that information made its way to your eyes before now?

Figure 1.3 iStock.com/SiberianArt

Source: https://www.istockphoto.com/faq/using-files#illustrations-and-vectors

Learning science has only just begun the process of sharing knowledge with the masses. For much of the history of learning science, results were disseminated primarily to other scientists by way of scientific journal articles. While this is important for moving science forward, these articles are not terribly accessible. Most of them exist behind a paywall and are written with lots of scientific jargon. Only recently have individuals started making concerted efforts to share their understanding of human learning with individuals that need help improving their learning.

The field to which most dissemination efforts are aimed is education. There have been several books written for educators (e.g., *Make It Stick*,[14] *Understanding How We Learn: A Visual Guide*,[9] *Powerful Teaching*[15]) and students (e.g., *Ace That Test: A Student's Guide to Learning Better*,[5] *Study Like a Champ*[16]). Several cognitive psychologists host websites (e.g., *learningscientists.org; retrievalpractice.org*) or podcasts (e.g., *The Learning Scientists Podcast*) about learning science. And many of these individuals engage in direct communication with educators through social media, talks, and workshops that span from primary through higher and medical education.

However, there has been considerably less outreach into other domains, despite the clear applicability and promise that learning science can provide.[17] This is particularly true in the context of organizational settings, where learning science can profoundly impact the entire talent cycle—from acquisition, management, retention, to exits.

- **In Talent Acquisition**, integrating learning science principles enhances onboarding, accelerating skill acquisition and fostering deeper cultural integration, underpinning the themes of "Strategic Talent Sourcing" and "Optimized Onboarding Experience."
- **During Talent Management**, incorporating insights from learning science enhances employee well-being and cultivates a positive organizational culture. This aligns with themes such as "Leadership Development and Career Pathing," and "Fostering Organizational Culture and Employee Well-being."
- **For Talent Retention**, prioritizing "Enhancing Employee Engagement" and emphasizing "Learning and Development" is crucial. This strategy ensures a supportive work culture, continuous skill enhancement, and clear career progression paths, fostering long-term loyalty and organizational success.
- **Even in Talent Exits**, organizations can adopt a dual approach focusing on "Operational Continuity and Knowledge Preservation" alongside "Alumni and Network Development." By leveraging learning science principles including social learning and continuous learning, alumni networks can serve as valuable resources for recruitment, mentorship, and knowledge transfer.

Just as with classroom settings, most organizations engage in some amount of formal learning. For example, most organizations train new employees through either formal classroom learning, webinars, etc. The work that has been done to disseminate learning science to classroom settings needs only be tweaked a bit to apply to these formal learning situations in organizations. But learning science can also be applied to informal situations as well. Learning science can inform how to better engage in actionable conversations, send impactful emails, and create long-lasting messages.

The big difference between classrooms and organizations? The motivation of the learners.

Motivation (or engagement) is one of the most critical first steps to learning and it's something that we'll discuss in detail throughout the book. The cognitive processes that lead to the best learning don't change as we grow into adulthood, but our background knowledge and motivation often do. Therefore throughout this book, we will consider the many ways that learning science has been used in classroom settings layered with the differences that you might see in your employees to create flexible principles that you can use to improve operations at your organization.

The Cycle Explored: Journey Ahead

As we wrap up this introductory chapter, it is evident that the potential of learning science extends well beyond academic confines. Its application in organizational contexts, particularly in the talent lifecycle, presents a transformative opportunity that remains largely untapped. Learning science provides a unique perspective to reevaluate and enhance the core processes of talent acquisition, management, retention, and exits within organizations.

We have traced the evolution of learning science, from its academic roots to its current status as an accessible, practical toolset for organizational improvement. This shift from a purely scholarly pursuit to a more

Figure 1.4 iStock.com/Olga Ubirailo
Source: https://www.istockphoto.com/faq/using-files#illustrations-and-vectors

applied approach opens up new avenues for companies to leverage these insights for both operational efficiency and employee development.

A critical aspect of applying learning science in an organizational setting lies in understanding the unique characteristics of adult learners. Unlike traditional educational environments, the corporate world deals with individuals who have varied motivations, experiences, and learning backgrounds. By customizing learning and development strategies to align with these factors, organizations can significantly enhance the effectiveness of their training programs, leading to increased employee engagement and satisfaction.

As we proceed to the next chapter, our focus will shift to an in-depth examination of the talent lifecycle. Each stage will be dissected and analyzed through the lens of learning science, offering practical, actionable insights and strategies. We will explore the interconnectedness of these stages and how a nuanced understanding of learning principles can transform each aspect of the talent cycle into a catalyst for organizational growth, efficiency, and innovation.

Our journey ahead is more than a theoretical discourse; it is about practical application in real-world settings. We aim to make a tangible impact on how organizations operate and flourish. This journey is not just about learning concepts; it is about redefining the future of work and learning, shaping how organizations grow and succeed.

References

1 Ebbinghaus, H. (1885/1964). *Memory: A contribution to experimental psychology.* Dover Publications.
2 Perlmutter, H. V., & De Montmollin, G. (1952). Group learning of nonsense syllables. *Journal of Abnormal and Social Psychology, 47*(4), 762.
3 Roediger, H. L., & McDermott, K. B. (1995). Creating false memories: Remembering words not presented in lists. *Journal of Experimental Psychology: Learning, Memory, and Cognition, 21*(4), 803.
4 Thorndike, E. L. (1908). Memory for paired associates. *Psychological Review, 15*(2), 122.
5 Sumeracki, M., Nebel, C., Kuepper-Tetzel, C., & Kaminske, A. N. (2023). *Ace that test: A student's guide to learning better.* David Fulton, Routledge.
6 Nguyen, C. D., & Boers, F. (2019). The effect of content retelling on vocabulary uptake from a TED talk. *Tesol Quarterly, 53*(1), 5–29.

7   Roediger III, H. L., & Karpicke, J. D. (2006). Test-enhanced learning: Taking memory tests improves long-term retention. *Psychological Science, 17*(3), 249–255.

8   Blumen, H. M., & Rajaram, S. (2009). Effects of repeated collaborative retrieval on individual memory vary as a function of recall versus recognition tasks. *Memory, 17*(8), 840–846.

9   Weinstein, Y., & Sumeracki, M. (2018). *Understanding how we learn: A visual guide.* Routledge.

10 Karpicke, J. D., & Bauernschmidt, A. (2011). Spaced retrieval: Absolute spacing enhances learning regardless of relative spacing. *Journal of Experimental Psychology: Learning, Memory, and Cognition, 37*(5), 1250.

11 Sumeracki, M. A., & Castillo, J. (2022). Covert and overt retrieval practice in the classroom. *Translational Issues in Psychological Science, 8*(2), 282.

12 Karpicke, J. D., Blunt, J. R., & Smith, M. A. (2016). Retrieval-based learning: Positive effects of retrieval practice in elementary school children. *Frontiers in Psychology, 7,* 350.

13 Deng, F., Gluckstein, J. A., & Larsen, D. P. (2015). Student-directed retrieval practice is a predictor of medical licensing examination performance. *Perspectives on Medical Education, 4,* 308–313.

14 Brown, P. C., Roediger III, H. L., & McDaniel, M. A. (2014). *Make it stick: The science of successful learning.* Harvard University Press.

15 Agarwal, P. K., & Bain, P. M. (2019). *Powerful teaching: Unleash the science of learning.* John Wiley & Sons.

16 Gurung, R. A., & Dunlosky, J. (2023). *Study like a champ: The psychology-based guide to "grade A" study habits.* American Psychological Association.

17 Sumeracki, M. A., Nebel, C. L., Kaminske, A. N., & Kuepper-Tetzel, C. E. (2024). Turning roadblocks into speed bumps: A call for implementation reform in science communication about retrieval practice. *Educational Psychology Review, 36*(1), 1–16.

2 | Talent Cycle Explained: The What

Figure 2.1 iStock.com/nickylarson974

Source: https://www.istockphoto.com/faq/using-files#illustrations-and-vectors

In the intricate world of managing organizations, we invite you to explore the intriguing concept of the talent cycle. Much like an enthralling novel filled with twists and turns, the talent cycle is a comprehensive voyage,

DOI: 10.4324/9781032711591-2

commencing with the meticulous process of scouting and welcoming new talents, followed by nurturing them through targeted training, and culminating in their flourishing careers within the organization or their eventual departure to new ventures. As we navigate this journey, we encounter various challenges and triumphs, reflecting the dynamic nature of human resources and organizational development. By intertwining learning science with the talent cycle, we aim to transform these challenges into opportunities for growth and innovation.

Before we delve into these challenges, it's crucial to establish a mutual understanding of what they entail. The concept of the talent cycle, often synonymous with the employee lifecycle, has been explored through various well-established frameworks. For example, the 6 Stages of the Talent Management Lifecycle, as outlined in Software Advice, categorizes the process into recruitment and attraction, onboarding, performance management, employee development, retention, and succession planning. This framework underscores the importance of each phase in building and maintaining a strong workforce.[1] Similarly, the Field Engineer's model of Talent Management Life Cycle emphasizes comprehensive stages such as talent acquisition, employee onboarding and orientation, performance management and employee development, and employee retention and succession planning. This model highlights the vital role of each stage in nurturing and retaining talent within an organization.[2]

Building on these insights, our book introduces *the talent cycle*, a unique model that segments employment into four key phases: talent acquisition, management, retention, and exits. Within each phase, we dissect various events, providing a granular view of the employee journey. It's important to note that our exploration is not an exhaustive examination of the talent cycle. Instead, we synthesize many existing concepts in the talent cycle and explore principles of learning science to enhance their effectiveness. There are domains in which learning science may not directly apply, such as benefit selection or how to increase belonging, which, although crucial, are beyond the scope of this book. Our primary objective is to deconstruct the talent cycle into an organized and understandable format, presenting strategies to tackle prevalent challenges using the lens of learning science.

Talent Acquisition

Our journey begins with discussing the first phase in the cycle, talent acquisition. Talent acquisition is the beginning of our story, the crucial first chapter where organizations embark on a quest to discover new members for their team. More than just filling positions, it's an ongoing strategy crucial for an organization's growth and future success.[3] Finding the right people can often feel like a formidable challenge, akin to searching for a pot of gold at the end of a rainbow. In fact, 75% of HR professionals report a skills gap among their applicants, making this quest even more intricate.[4]

This phase is more than just a hunt for talent; it's about aligning new hires with an organization's ethos and future goals. Given that more than 90% of employers are hiring for new roles, the landscape of talent acquisition is both dynamic and demanding.[4] We are also witnessing a historic shift in the workforce, with a record-high talent gap and increasing voluntary resignations adding to the complexity of this task.[5]

Figure 2.2 Source: iStock.com/designer491

Source: https://www.istockphoto.com/faq/using-files#illustrations-and-vectors

As we move forward, we'll explore the common problems that come with talent acquisition. We'll delve into strategies to navigate these challenges, leveraging learning science to transform talent acquisition from an endless chase into a structured, successful journey.

Problem 1: High Recruitment Costs and Lengthy Hiring Cycles

As we delve into the complexities of talent acquisition, a formidable hurdle emerges: the combined challenge of high recruitment costs and protracted hiring cycles. This issue, intensified by the 75% of HR professionals recognizing a skills gap among applicants, not only affects fiscal resources but also impacts organizational agility and efficiency.[4] The financial implications are striking. According to the Society for Human Resource Management (SHRM), the average cost of hiring a new employee can reach up to $4,700, with some estimates suggesting that that could swell to three to four times the employee's annual salary. This underscores the substantial investment companies make in recruitment and the importance of retention strategies to mitigate these costs. This is akin to spending a small fortune in pursuit of that elusive "perfect" candidate.[6] Moreover, the time investment is equally significant. Research by Glassdoor indicates that U.S. companies average 23.8 days in the interview process, transforming a streamlined procedure into a drawn-out saga.[7]

But here's where the principles of learning science offer a glimmer of hope. Learning science, with its emphasis on data-driven decision-making and understanding human behavior and cognition, can be a game-changer in talent acquisition. By applying learning theories and analytics, organizations can streamline recruitment processes, better predict candidate success, and enhance the overall efficiency of talent sourcing.

Problem 2: Identifying Skills and Culture Alignment

The next intricate challenge in talent acquisition is twofold: accurately identifying essential soft skills and ensuring cultural alignment. In today's dynamic workplace, soft skills such as communication, adaptability, and teamwork are increasingly critical. Yet 68% of talent professionals struggle to assess these skills effectively during the recruitment process, leading to hires who may excel in technical prowess but falter in collaborative or adaptive capacities.[8] Compounding this issue is the high cost of poor hiring decisions, which are often linked to a lack of cultural fit. More than 80% of employee turnover stems from such flawed hiring choices,[8] which underscores the necessity of aligning new hires not just with the technical demands of a role but also with the company's core values and culture.

Another dimension to this challenge is the prevalent external bias in hiring. Data from *Harvard Business Review* indicates that only 28% of talent acquisition leaders view internal candidates as a significant source for filling vacancies.[9] This external-focused approach risks overlooking potential internal candidates who may offer a better cultural fit and have proved their value within the organization.

This is where the principles of learning science can pave the way to more effective solutions. Learning science can offer invaluable insights into both cultural fit and the development of more nuanced recruitment strategies. These strategies can include behaviorally anchored rating scales, realistic job previews, and structured interviews that focus not only on technical expertise but also on candidates' alignment with organizational values. By applying these principles, we can move beyond conventional recruitment methodologies, improving the accuracy of skill assessment and enhancing cultural alignment in hiring decisions.

Problem 3: Onboarding Challenges and High Turnover

Effective onboarding is not just a preliminary step but a cornerstone of organizational success. Yet, the current state of onboarding presents a significant challenge. Gallup's State of the Global Workplace report in 2017 revealed a startling reality: only 12% of employees strongly believe that their organizations excel in onboarding new hires. This statistic is a clear indication of the widespread inadequacy in the early stages of the talent cycle.[10]

The financial impact of poor onboarding is equally alarming. According to the Work Institute's 2020 Retention Report, the estimated cost of employee turnover in the United States is around a staggering $630 billion.[11] This highlights the crucial role of onboarding in not just welcoming new hires but in sustaining a stable, productive workforce. Contrasting this bleak picture is the promising finding that companies excelling in onboarding see a 91% employee retention rate in the first year of hiring.[12]

This is a testament to the transformative power of effective onboarding processes.

In the context of talent acquisition, organizations face distinct challenges that extend beyond merely filling positions. Talent acquisition today is about strategically sourcing candidates who align with the company's culture and have the potential for future growth. It involves navigating the complexities of identifying the right blend of skills and cultural fit, managing recruitment costs, and ensuring a smooth onboarding process. At this juncture, learning science principles offer insightful solutions to these onboarding challenges. By understanding how adults learn and adapt to new environments, learning science can inform the development of more effective, engaging onboarding programs.

The approach to these challenges can be categorized under two main themes: "strategic talent sourcing" and "optimized onboarding experience." The first theme focuses on the precision in identifying and attracting the right talent, considering both skillset and cultural alignment. The second theme emphasizes creating effective onboarding processes to integrate new hires seamlessly into the organization.

By implementing learning science principles in these areas, organizations can optimize their talent acquisition strategies, leading to a more effective, efficient, and employee-centric hiring process. Additionally, applying learning analytics can help tailor onboarding experiences to individual needs, thereby increasing engagement and reducing the likelihood of early turnover. By harnessing the power of learning science, organizations can transform their onboarding processes into a strategic asset, reducing turnover and cultivating a committed and competent workforce.

So, how do these potentially show up in the workforce?

Talent Acquisition Challenges in a Tech Company

Strategic Talent Sourcing—High Recruitment Costs and Lengthy Hiring Cycles

In a bustling tech company, the quest to recruit niche software developers like those skilled in TensorFlow and PyTorch mirrors a high-stakes treasure hunt. This process is costly and time consuming, with the discovery of such rare talent demanding a premium. This leads to stretched project timelines and waning competitiveness, reflecting the challenges of strategic talent sourcing in a rapidly evolving tech landscape.

Strategic Talent Sourcing—Skills and Cultural Alignment

Identifying candidates who possess both the necessary technical skills and a strong cultural fit within a company is a complex challenge. It's akin to finding a rare gem; the alignment of an individual's values, work style, and behavior with the company's culture is both crucial for long-term success and difficult to find. A culture clash occurs when there's a misalignment between the candidate's and the company's values, potentially leading to reduced job satisfaction, performance issues, and increased turnover.

Optimized Onboarding Experience—Addressing Turnover

In addition to bringing in talented individuals, the company faces a critical issue in onboarding. Considerable time is spent on new employee errors in areas that were covered during onboarding, indicating that employees are not retaining new knowledge and skills and putting a considerable strain on existing staff.

These scenarios illustrate the multifaceted challenges of talent acquisition in the tech company, from strategic sourcing to onboarding. This narrative not only illustrates the trials faced but vividly showcases their impact within the tech company's dynamic ecosystem. From the quest for skilled developers to the complex web of internal challenges, these issues collectively endangered the company's prosperity, employee morale, and capacity for innovation.

However, this is just the beginning of the talent acquisition saga. As we prepare to lift the curtain on the role of learning science in providing solutions, let us now embark on the next phase of our journey—venturing into the realm of talent management. Here, we will encounter a new set of challenges and opportunities, revealing the crucial role of effective management in nurturing and retaining talent.

Talent Management

Talent management is a strategic orchestration within an organization aimed at developing talented individuals to fulfill both current and future

Figure 2.3 iStock.com/EtiAmmos

Source: https://www.istockphoto.com/faq/using-files#illustrations-and-vectors

organizational needs. It is a multifaceted process that encompasses a range of practices that include training, performance management, and employee development, all designed to maximize the workforce's potential. In simpler terms, talent management is the roadmap and tool-kit used by an organization to nurture its most crucial asset—its people. This involves fostering their growth and success and ensuring they remain engaged, motivated, and aligned with the organization's objectives.

According to McKinsey, effective talent management includes shaping a skill strategy to ensure the workforce is future ready and shifting infra-structure for skilling at scale, ensuring a nearly 100% chance of success-ful skill transformation.[13] Valamis adds that talent management involves developing strategies for attracting, retaining, and transitioning employ-ees, ensuring they feel valued and motivated within the organization.

In the talent management phase, unique challenges arise when ensur-ing each member of a large group receives the appropriate training and opportunities. Yet, organizations often overlook the need for personalized development plans, and the training provided may not align with the company's strategic goals. Additionally, tracking employee performance and identifying areas for improvement can be complex. These challenges can lead to undesirable outcomes: employees feeling unengaged and unmotivated, ultimately leading to turnover.

Thus, talent management is not merely about assigning roles; it's about nurturing an organizational culture that supports employee well-being and work–life integration. This means creating an environment in which employees feel connected to the company's values, and where their holistic well-being is a priority. A positive organizational culture is essential for sustaining a motivated workforce and reducing burnout and turnover. It is about creating a journey that aligns employee growth with the company's vision, ensuring that each individual's path contributes meaningfully to the organizational tapestry. This includes focusing on leadership development, clear career pathing, fostering a strong organizational culture, and ensuring employee well-being. These elements work together to build a robust and sustainable talent management strategy that meets both the current and future needs of the organization.

Here are some major problems we have noticed in the talent management stage.

Problem 1: Developing Future Leaders

Talent management confronts a pivotal challenge: nurturing the leaders of tomorrow. In spite of the acknowledged importance of leadership development, there's a stark contrast between recognition and action. Zippia's research underscores this gap, revealing that while 83% of businesses recognize the importance of investing in leadership development for entry-level roles, only 5% have actively embarked on this transformative journey. This discrepancy hints at a major oversight in harnessing future leadership potential.[14,15]

Moreover, only 48% of employees view their company's leadership as "high quality," suggesting a disconnection between leadership perception and reality. It's as if organizations hold all the pieces of a leadership puzzle but struggle to assemble them into a coherent pattern for growth.[16] The concerns deepen when considering the findings of the 2023 Global Leadership Forecast by DDI, which reports a significant decline in leadership quality. The study reveals a 17% drop in leaders who believe their organizations possess high-quality leadership, now standing at just 40%—a figure nearly on par with those in the wake of the 2007–2008 economic crisis. This drop indicates a growing leadership crisis that could hinder organizational progress and stifle innovation.[17,18]

Addressing this imperative is not merely about filling leadership roles but about fostering a culture in which leadership development is prioritized. Effective nurturing of leadership talent is essential for retaining employees, elevating the skill set of the current staff, and shaping them into the leaders of tomorrow. It's a cornerstone in fortifying organizational leadership, essential for sustainable growth and adaptability in an ever-evolving landscape.

This leadership development conundrum, however, is precisely where learning science can play a transformative role. Learning science, with its insights into how adults acquire, retain, and apply knowledge and skills, offers invaluable tools for crafting effective leadership development programs. By integrating principles such as experiential learning, tailored learning pathways, and continuous feedback mechanisms, learning science can bridge the gap between potential and performance in emerging leaders.

Moreover, learning science emphasizes the importance of a growth mindset and the development of soft skills such as emotional intelligence and adaptive thinking—skills that are crucial for effective leadership in today's dynamic business environments. By fostering these competencies, organizations can cultivate a leadership pool that is not only technically proficient but also emotionally intelligent and agile.

In essence, the integration of learning science into leadership development strategies promises a more systematic, data-driven, and personalized approach. This alignment can transform the landscape of leadership development, turning the challenge of nurturing future leaders into an opportunity for building a robust, dynamic, and future-ready leadership bench.

Problem 2: Creating Clear Career Paths

One critical issue in talent management is the formulation of well-defined career paths for employees. Career paths are the planned routes within a company that enable employees to progress, take on more responsibilities, and achieve their career goals. They serve as a navigational chart for career growth and success. However, Gartner's research in March 2022 reveals a troubling gap: fewer than one in three employees has a clear understanding of how to progress their career over the next 5 years within their organization.[19] The absence of clear career direction resembles embarking on a voyage without a compass, leaving both journey and destination uncertain. The absence of clear career paths can subtly erode motivation and engagement, potentially leading to talent attrition. Well-defined career paths not only ignite motivation but also guide employees' individual growth in alignment with organizational objectives.

Learning science can play a crucial role in addressing this challenge. By leveraging principles such as personalized learning paths, competency-based development, and continuous learning, learning science can help create clear and flexible career pathways. It enables organizations to map out career trajectories that are not only aligned with business needs but also cater to individual employee aspirations. This approach not only enhances career satisfaction but also bolsters the overall talent management strategy.

Problem 3: Fostering Organizational Culture and Employee Well-being

In the sphere of talent management, the cultivation of a positive organizational culture and the assurance of employee well-being are not just beneficial but essential. These factors significantly influence employee satisfaction and motivation as evidenced by various studies and statistics. For example, research underscores the critical role of effective management in enhancing employee well-being and experience. Poor management significantly raises the likelihood of employees seeking new opportunities, while clear communication regarding roles and responsibilities can increase their inclination to stay. This emphasizes the necessity of cultivating a supportive work culture that prioritizes clear communication and employee well-being, rather than focusing solely on retention metrics.[20]

Developing an organizational culture that mirrors the company's values and goals, while integrating employee well-being into the organizational structure, is a significant challenge. It's crucial for creating an environment in which employees feel valued and supported. In support of this, statistics reveal that 58% of employees would prefer to stay at a lower paying job if it meant working for a great boss, underscoring the value placed on positive workplace relationships over compensation.[20]

Furthermore, learning science offers insights into enhancing employee well-being and building a positive organizational culture. Principles such as fostering a sense of community, offering recognition, and supporting work–life balance are vital. They contribute to a healthier, more productive workplace. In line with this, flexible work arrangements have become increasingly important, with 76% of employees seeking jobs offering more flexibility to maintain a healthy work–life balance. Moreover, 77% believe flexible work options would enable them to lead healthier lives, and 86% think such arrangements would reduce their stress levels.[20]

The challenges within talent management can be effectively restructured into two primary themes: leadership development and career pathing and fostering organizational culture and employee well-being. The first theme ensures that employees are equipped with essential leadership skills and have a clear understanding of their potential growth and progression within the organization. The second theme places a strong emphasis on building a work environment that aligns with the company's values and goals, and emphasizes the importance of employee health, satisfaction, and overall well-being. Together, these themes form a comprehensive strategy in talent management, focusing not only on professional growth and career development but also on cultivating a supportive and nurturing workplace culture.

By prioritizing these elements, organizations can create a culture that attracts and retains top talent. The integration of learning science principles in fostering a positive organizational culture and employee well-being promises a more systematic, tailored, and effective approach. This strategic focus leads to a more effective, fulfilling, and sustainable talent management process, ensuring a stable and thriving workforce.

As we refine our exploration of talent management challenges to fit the updated themes, let's re-envision a scenario within a fictional marketing company. This setting will provide us with a practical framework to understand how these challenges might manifest.

Talent Management Challenges in a Marketing Company

Leadership Development and Career Pathing—Nurturing Future Leaders and Defining Career Trajectories

In a bustling marketing firm, a talented group of young account managers shows promise but struggles with unclear advancement paths. They're eager to progress into senior roles but lack guidance on the necessary qualifications or steps. Meanwhile, the firm's creative department feels disconnected from the company's recent shift towards data-driven marketing strategies, feeling their creativity is undervalued. These scenarios highlight the need for a structured leadership development program and clearer career paths that align with both the evolving company values and the diverse aspirations of its employees.

Fostering Organizational Culture and Employee Well-being

In the same marketing firm, there's a deeper issue of disconnect between employees and the company's evolving data-driven focus. This misalignment extends beyond career paths to affect the firm's culture and employee well-being. The creative team, feeling undervalued, highlights a broader problem of employees struggling to find their place in the company's future direction, impacting their job satisfaction and productivity. This scenario stresses the need for nurturing an organizational culture that equally values employee well-being and aligns with the company's strategic goals.

These fictional scenarios mirror common situations in many organizations, illustrating the complexities of talent management. They span across the spectrums of leadership development, career path clarity, organizational culture, and employee well-being. In the subsequent chapters, we will delve into how learning science can provide effective strategies and solutions to these challenges. We will also examine the integral role of talent retention in the talent cycle, demonstrating how these elements interconnect to create a cohesive and effective talent management strategy.

Talent Retention

Holding onto exceptional talent in an organization is often compared to an arduous uphill climb. Talent retention is crucially defined as an organization's ability to keep its employees, especially the best ones. It involves strategies to prevent top talent from leaving, as losing skilled employees can be both costly and disruptive to the organization's progress. A strong retention strategy not only combats voluntary turnover but also supports the organization's long-term growth and stability.[21] Talent management and retention are inextricably linked but while management is focused on enhancing the productivity of the current employees, retention is focused on keeping them.

Figure 2.4 iStock.com/Vectors Tank

Source: https://www.istockphoto.com/faq/using-files#illustrations-and-vectors

In this landscape, the challenge of retaining talent looms large. Many organizations grapple with high turnover rates, akin to a situation where rivals are persistently attempting to lure away their brightest stars. This often results in an unsettling sense of undervaluation and underappreciation among employees, exacerbated by limited opportunities for career advancement and skill enhancement. Consequently, this creates a formidable obstacle in maintaining a stable and committed workforce.

As we delve into the intricacies of talent retention, we recognize that it is a critical component of organizational success. While understanding its importance is the first step, it's equally crucial to identify and address the specific challenges that arise in this area. The next section will explore these challenges, shedding light on the common issues organizations face in retaining their valuable talent. We will dissect the various factors that contribute to high turnover rates and the strategies needed to mitigate these problems, ensuring a stable and engaged workforce.

Problem 1: Competitor Poaching

One persistent challenge in talent retention is the lure of competitors attempting to entice an organization's top talent away. This competition for talent is intense, as highlighted by new research published by Zippia, which reveals that 73% of the job-seeking market is composed of passive candidates. Among these, many are open to exploring new opportunities, especially when actively recruited by others. Furthermore, the Work Institute's 2020 Retention Report indicates that about 38% of employees decide to leave their organization within their first year, with those leaving within the initial 90 days providing little return on the investment made in hiring and onboarding them.[22]

Learning science can provide valuable insights into this challenge. By understanding the factors that drive employee satisfaction and commitment, organizations can develop targeted strategies to enhance employee engagement and loyalty. Techniques such as personalized learning and development plans, recognition of achievements, and fostering a positive organizational culture can make an organization more attractive to its employees, thereby reducing the risk of them being enticed away by competitors.

Problem 2: Undervaluation and Discontent

Another critical challenge in talent retention is employee morale and job satisfaction. Employees often feel undervalued and unappreciated, leading to disengagement and a desire for new opportunities. According to the Work Institute's 2022 Retention Report, one of the primary reasons employees leave is the lack of recognition and appreciation in the workplace. This situation can be likened to working tirelessly on a project only for it to go unnoticed, leading to a sense of futility and discouragement.[23]

Learning science offers solutions to this challenge by emphasizing the importance of personalized recognition and positive feedback. By applying principles such as meaningful recognition, organizations can create an environment where employees feel valued for their contributions. This approach not only boosts morale but also fosters a culture of appreciation, significantly enhancing employee retention.

Problem 3: Limited Growth Opportunities

The perception of limited avenues for skill development and career advancement is a significant contributor to talent attrition. A notable finding from a LinkedIn workplace learning report is that 94% of employees are more likely to stay longer at a company that invests in their career growth.[24] This statistic highlights the critical importance of providing clear opportunities for professional development. Without visible pathways for advancement, employees may feel like they're navigating their careers without a map, leading to frustration and a higher likelihood of seeking opportunities elsewhere.

Learning science can help address this challenge by emphasizing the importance of continuous learning and skill development. By creating tailored development programs and clear career progression pathways, organizations can foster an environment where employees feel valued and see a future, thus enhancing retention rates.[24,25]

Holding onto exceptional talent in modern organizations involves addressing complex challenges beyond just competitive offerings. Employees seek a harmonious blend of work–life balance, opportunities for career growth, recognition, and an inclusive environment. Organizations not meeting these needs face the risk of talent attrition, manifesting in various forms such as competitor poaching, undervaluation, and limited growth opportunities.

The response to these challenges lies in a two-pronged approach: enhancing employee engagement and focusing on learning and development. Employee engagement addresses the need for recognition, inclusivity, and a supportive work culture. Learning and development emphasizes continuous skill enhancement and clear career progression paths. Integrating these elements is key to fostering long-term employee loyalty and success.

Talent Retention Challenges in a Mid-sized Manufacturing Company

Employee Engagement—the Battle Against Competitor Poaching

In a manufacturing company facing high turnover, especially among upper level employees, exit interviews reveal that competitive pay and benefits from rivals are key reasons for departures. The turnover rate, notably higher for senior staff, underscores the urgency of enhancing employee engagement and fostering a culture where employees feel deeply connected to the company's mission, beyond financial incentives. This detailed scenario points to the need for a strategic approach to employee retention that addresses the core issues identified through feedback.

Recognition and Morale—Tackling Undervaluation and Discontent

Over time, employees increasingly feel undervalued and overlooked, resulting in a noticeable decline in morale across the organization. This concerning trend highlights the critical importance of implementing a comprehensive employee recognition program. By actively acknowledging and celebrating employees' efforts and achievements, the company can boost morale, improve job satisfaction, and foster a more positive work environment where employees feel appreciated and motivated to excel.

Learning and Development—Addressing Stagnation in Skill Development and Career Advancement

A recent employee survey revealed a concerning trend: a significant portion of employees express uncertainty about their career advancement prospects within the company. This lack of clarity and limited opportunities for skill development contribute to a sense of professional stagnation among the workforce. To combat this issue, it's imperative to prioritize learning and development initiatives aimed at providing clear pathways for career growth and continuous skill enhancement. By investing in employees' professional development, the company not only equips them with the skills needed to excel in their roles but also demonstrates a commitment to their long-term success and fulfillment.

Before exploring learning science-based solutions, the next section delves into the final stage of the talent cycle: talent exits, highlighting its significance in talent management.

Talent Exits

The concept of talent exits is a crucial part of the employee lifecycle. In simple terms, talent exits refer to the processes and strategies employed by organizations when employees decide to move on from their roles

Figure 2.5 iStock.com/Aleutie

Source: https://www.istockphoto.com/faq/using-files#illustrations-and-vectors

within the company. This often overlooked phase is critical for maintaining continuity, preserving institutional knowledge, and ensuring a smooth transition as employees depart and new talent takes their place. Research indicates that turnover costs can vary significantly, spanning from 25% to a staggering 500% of an employee's annual compensation. On average, the departure of a single employee can incur an estimated cost of $13,996 to the organization. These costs encompass various expenses associated with employee turnover, including recruitment and hiring expenses, training costs for new hires, productivity losses during the transition period, and potential impacts on team morale and overall organizational performance. Understanding the substantial financial implications of employee turnover underscores the importance of implementing effective retention strategies to minimize these costs and maintain a stable and productive workforce.[26] Understanding and effectively managing talent exits are crucial for organizations to mitigate these financial implications, preserving institutional knowledge, and maintaining operational continuity.

Common problems in this stage include the following.

Problem 1: Knowledge Gaps and Disruptions

One of the key challenges within talent exits is the potential for knowledge gaps and operational disruptions. When employees leave without proper knowledge transfer, it's like missing pages from a manual needed to operate a complex machine. These gaps can hinder productivity, create inefficiencies, and negatively impact the quality of work. According to a study by the SHRM, 75% of professionals consider knowledge transfer important.[27] However, the latest edition of Deloitte's Global Human Capital Trends study ranks "knowledge management" as one of the top three issues influencing company success, yet only 9% of surveyed organizations feel ready to address it.[28] The departure of experienced team members can be particularly concerning, as their expertise and institutional knowledge walk out of the door with them. Learning science can help by informing optimized knowledge-sharing processes, ensuring organization continuity and reducing the impact of these gaps.

Problem 2: Insufficient Succession Planning

Effective succession planning is an integral part of talent exits. However, many organizations struggle in this area. Succession planning is like having a well-thought-out game plan for the future, ensuring that when key individuals depart, there are capable team members ready to step into their shoes. Without robust succession plans, companies may find themselves in a state of flux, scrambling to fill critical roles and maintain operational continuity. In a survey by Deloitte, only 14% of organizations believed they had an excellent succession plan in place, highlighting the widespread challenge.[29] Learning science principles, such as expertise effects and storytelling, can enhance succession planning by maximizing the transfer of knowledge and skills to the succeeding employee.

Problem 3: Underutilization of Alumni Networks and Resources

A key challenge in the talent exit process is the underutilization of alumni networks and resources. Research indicates that alumni play a critical role in the growth and development of their former institutions. Their engagement can bring myriad benefits, from serving as role models and mentors to providing expertise and aiding in recruitment efforts. However, many organizations fail to effectively engage their alumni, missing out on the opportunity to leverage this valuable resource. Alumni can contribute significantly to institutional governance, support in student recruitment, and enhancement of the reputation of the organization. Addressing this challenge involves developing strategies to actively engage alumni, creating channels for their continued involvement, and recognizing their potential contributions to the organization's growth and success.[30]

Learning science can inform the benefits of alumni networks and resources. By applying principles such as diversity of thought, social learning, and spaced review, organizations can see the power and potential of alumni networks for recruitment and mentorship. Additionally, learning science emphasizes the importance of continuous learning, which can be fostered through alumni-led workshops or webinars, effectively keeping the alumni connected and actively contributing to the organization's knowledge base and culture.

In addressing the challenges of talent exits, we can reframe them under two main themes: operational continuity and knowledge preservation and alumni and network development. These categories cover the crucial aspects of knowledge transfer and maintaining connections post-exit.

Addressing these challenges is key to ensuring smooth transitions, preserving institutional knowledge, and maintaining a connected community. This approach involves not only managing the exits but also leveraging the expertise and networks of former employees for ongoing organizational development.

To further paint how this may look in the workforce, here is a manifestation.

Talent Exit Challenges in Manufacturing Company

Operational Continuity and Knowledge Preservation

The departure of senior engineers poses a critical challenge for the manufacturing company, particularly concerning operational continuity and knowledge preservation. With their exit, the organization experiences substantial knowledge gaps, losing decades of industry insights and problem-solving expertise. The absence of robust knowledge transfer systems exacerbates the situation, leaving the remaining workforce ill-equipped to fill these significant voids and maintain seamless operations.

Alumni and Network Development

The company grapples with the challenge of maintaining meaningful connections with former employees. Inefficient alumni engagement processes result in missed opportunities to tap into their valuable expertise and expansive networks for ongoing organizational support. This lack of engagement not only hampers the company's operational capabilities but also dilutes its cultural heritage. Alumni, as former insiders, possess invaluable insights and experiences that can enrich the organization's decision-making processes, mentor current employees, and uphold its legacy.

In this context, the organization recognizes that managing talent exits transcends mere departure logistics; it entails strategically harnessing the knowledge and networks of former employees for sustained growth and resilience. For instance, as the company considers expansion into new markets, the insights of former top talents could prove invaluable in shaping strategic decisions. Similarly, when recruiting new talent, leveraging the connections of former employees working in relevant sectors could significantly boost recruitment efforts. Yet, the lack of ongoing communication makes initiating such conversations uncomfortable and impractical.

In this scenario, the organization acknowledges that effectively managing talent exits entails more than just handling departures; it's also about strategically leveraging the knowledge and networks of former employees to foster continued growth and resilience.

Moving Forward

With a comprehensive understanding of the entire talent cycle, we are now ready to explore how learning science can innovatively address these challenges. Our next step is to delve into the application of learning science principles across the talent cycle, starting with talent acquisition, and moving through to talent exits, to create a holistic and effective talent management strategy, and enhance existing strategies.

References

1 https://www.softwareadvice.com/resources/talent-management-life-cycle/
2 https://www.fieldengineer.com/article/talent-management-lifecycle/
3 https://www.valamis.com/hub/talent-acquisition
4 https://www.instride.com/insights/talent-acquisition-recruitment-statistics/
5 https://www.brazen.com/resources/talent-acquisition-stats
6 https://www.shrm.org/topics-tools/news/talent-acquisition/real-costs-recruitment
7 https://www.glassdoor.com/research/time-to-hire-in-25-countries
8 https://business.linkedin.com/content/dam/me/business/en-us/talent-solutions/resources/pdfs/global_talent_trends_2019_emea.pdf
9 https://hbr.org/2019/05/your-approach-to-hiring-is-all-wrong
10 https://www.gallup.com/workplace/247172/problems-onboarding-program.aspx#:~:text=Only%2012%25%20of%20employees%20strongly,engagement%20among%20employees%20who%20stay
11 https://info.workinstitute.com/hubfs/2020%20Retention%20Report/Work%20Institutes%202020%20Retention%20Report.pdf
12 https://www.shrm.org/topics-tools/news/hr-magazine/original-onboarding-options-4-hr-leaders
13 https://www.mckinsey.com/featured-insights/mckinsey-explainers/what-is-talent-management
14 https://edainc.io/what-are-the-latest-leadership-development-trends/
15 https://www.keka.com/glossary/leadership-development
16 https://www.zippia.com/advice/leadership-statistics/
17 https://www.ddiworld.com/global-leadership-forecast-2023
18 https://www.ddiworld.com/about/media/global-leadership-forecast-2023
19 https://influencing.com/pr/104940/gartner-hr-research-finds-just-25-of-employees-are-confident-about-their-career-at-their-current-organisation
20 https://builtin.com/company-culture/company-culture-statistics
21 https://www.quantumworkplace.com/future-of-work/why-employee-retention-is-important
22 https://www.apcinc.com/2022/09/22/new-statistics-on-passive-candidates/
23 https://info.workinstitute.com/2022-retention-report
24 https://learning.linkedin.com/resources/workplace-learning-report-2018
25 https://partners.pennfoster.edu/blog/2022/february/the-importance-of-talent-development-in-todays-labor-market
26 https://sajhrm.co.za/index.php/sajhrm/article/view/873

27 https://www.shrm.org/topics-tools/news/hr-magazine/capture-what-employees-know-before-they-leave-the-company

28 https://www2.deloitte.com/xe/en/insights/focus/technology-and-the-future-of-work//organizational-knowledge-management.html

29 https://action.deloitte.com/insight/1874/how-to-put-the-success-in-succession

30 Obeng-Ofori, D., & Kwarteng, H. O. (2021). Enhancing the role of alumni in the growth of higher education institutions. *International Journal of Multidisciplinary Studies and Innovative Research, 4,* 40–48.

3 | Talent Acquisition

Figure 3.1 iStock.com/designer491
Source: https://www.istockphoto.com/faq/using-files#illustrations-and-vectors

In the ever-shifting maze of talent acquisition, companies face a hydra of challenges so formidable it makes finding the office coffee machine seem like child's play. Human resources professionals must expertly navigate this maze, which includes not only the tangible aspects of hiring—like the financial headaches and logistical hoop-jumping—but also the more

DOI: 10.4324/9781032711591-3

whimsical pathways of cultural alignment, employee engagement, and getting everyone to agree on which office snack is best.

In this age of rapid technological evolution, the ancient maps of talent acquisition are as outdated as floppy disks. Companies now realize that hiring talent is not a straight line, but a multidimensional quest that requires a strategic fusion of data-driven insights, a touch of psychology, and a sprinkle of innovative foresight.

As we venture deeper, we encounter various mystical entities shaping the talent acquisition landscape. Here are a few fictional concepts addressing real issues:

The Chameleon's Dilemma: Just like a chameleon changes its colors to adapt to different environments, companies face the challenge of adapting to the evolving expectations of a diverse pool of candidates. It's not just about ticking the boxes of diversity; it's about truly understanding and embracing the multifaceted needs and aspirations of candidates from various backgrounds. In a straightforward sense, this means constantly updating recruitment strategies to be as welcoming and accommodating as possible, ensuring everyone feels valued and represented.

The Techno-Mage's Conundrum: Imagine a wizard who's traded in the ancient spellbook for a sleek laptop, fusing the old-school magic of human intuition with the latest AI and machine learning technology in recruitment. This conundrum represents the challenge of integrating advanced technology into the hiring process, without losing the human touch. In practical terms, it's about using data-driven insights to enhance decision-making, while still valuing the irreplaceable human elements of empathy and understanding in recruitment.

The Siren's Call: Just as the mythical sirens lured sailors with their enchanting music, a company's employer brand has the power to attract or repel potential candidates. This concept is about navigating the delicate balance between showcasing the company's strengths and culture and maintaining authenticity in how it's presented to the world. A strong employer brand isn't just about singing your own praises; it's about creating a genuine and appealing candidate experience that resonates with the values and aspirations of potential employees.

The Agile Griffin: In a world where the only constant is change, recruitment strategies need to be as agile and versatile as a griffin in flight. This means being open to new ideas, swiftly adapting to market changes, and being ready to pivot strategies at a moment's notice. It's about creating a recruitment process that's not only robust but also capable of soaring through the unpredictable winds of the talent market.

In this realm of complexities, two principal themes illuminate the path through our main challenges: 1) strategic talent sourcing and 2) optimized onboarding. Our journey through talent acquisition will not only examine the challenges above but also reveal practical strategies for growth and success, grounded in learning science. By harnessing these principles, organizations can transform their hiring processes into strategic assets, reducing turnover and cultivating a competent and committed workforce.

Strategic Talent Sourcing

Strategic talent sourcing is not only a financial balancing act; it also involves the delicate art of ensuring cultural harmony within an organization. This challenge is intertwined with the financial aspects of hiring, as a misalignment in cultural fit can lead to increased turnover, further escalating recruitment costs. As mentioned in Chapter 2, the Society of Human Resource Management (SHRM) estimates that the average cost-per-hire exceeds $4,000, sometimes amounting to three to four times the salary of the position.[1] These costs encompass a range of direct and indirect expenses, each contributing to the overall financial burden. Direct costs include advertising, staff time for reviewing applications and conducting interviews, and the onboarding of new hires. Indirect expenses, often less visible, involve training costs and lost productivity during vacancies. When positions remain unfilled, such as a key role in a tech company, the ramifications can be significant, including delayed projects, revenue losses, and a buildup of hiring costs. Understanding and integrating a candidate's alignment with company culture is a nuanced process, crucial for long-term organizational health and financial sustainability. The cost of a cultural misfit extends beyond immediate hiring expenses to encompass productivity loss, morale issues, and increased turnover. Assessing cultural fit during recruitment is

Figure 3.2 iStock.com/Visual Generation

Source: https://www.istockphoto.com/faq/using-files#illustrations-and-vectors

thus vital, involving structured interviews and behavioral assessments that evaluate a candidate's alignment with the company's ethos.

In response to these challenges, enhancing the candidate experience emerges as a vital strategy. By applying learning science principles, organizations can craft interactions that resonate with candidates, fostering engagement and streamlining the recruitment funnel.

The Science Behind Strategic Talent Sourcing

Strategic talent sourcing leverages a synergy of data analytics and psychological understanding. Data analytics, particularly predictive analytics, is crucial for anticipating hiring needs and discerning market trends. This enables organizations to take a proactive stance in talent acquisition, staying ahead of industry shifts. The psychological aspect focuses on grasping candidate motivations, behaviors, and cultural compatibility.

At the heart of this approach is the application of learning science principles, which are instrumental in optimizing the recruitment process, including enhancing candidate experience and ensuring the right individuals become employees. The factors below have the potential to impact talent sourcing, although not all of them are critical all of the time. We have tried to describe the science behind each concept with concrete applications of when they might be most useful.

Candidate Motivation

In Chapter 5, we do a deep dive into employee motivation. Here, however, we will describe the factors that are most likely to impact whether or not a candidate chooses to apply to an organization, from a learning science lens.

Cognitive Load and Self-Efficacy

For candidates to persist beyond the point of seeing a job opening to applying, they need to feel confident that they can successfully apply and ultimately be hired. While this seems straightforward, many applications are written in such a way that limits the number of applicants. This is partially due to our finite attentional systems, our working memory. When an applicant has to use a lot of brain power to decipher the text in an application, it makes the job itself sound much more demanding.[2] Potential applicants may also have a difficult time deciding if they are a good candidate due to the jargon used to describe the position, which can lead to uncertainty about the details of the position. If they are unsure if the time invested in applying will lead to an interview or hire, they are far less likely to persist with actually applying. This is related to the concept of self-efficacy, our belief in our ability to succeed at any given task.[3] If we can reduce the cognitive load associated with understanding applications, we can increase the self-efficacy of potential applicants, making them more likely to apply.

Spaced Review

Sometimes after applications are submitted, a lot of time can go by before interviews or hires occur. And in today's environment, candidates can be waiting to hear back about dozens of applications. To keep candidates interested, engaged, and to simply remember the position of interest, the principle of spaced review can be utilized. Spaced review is the idea that information is much better remembered when we are reminded of it over time.[4] We will go into this in more detail later in this chapter in the section on onboarding, but for applicants, making sure that they have touchpoints throughout the talent sourcing process can be useful to keep their interest in your organization top of mind.

Cultural Fit: Development of Understanding

A critical issue in hiring new candidates is ensuring that they fit with the culture and mission of the organization. Communicating information about the culture of the organization is key to making sure the right candidates apply. Several strategies can be used to improve the understanding of the cultural fit of new hires.

Concrete Examples[5]

When describing abstract ideas about company culture, it can be difficult for candidates to understand exactly what those abstract ideas mean in the context of day-to-day work. For example, maybe your organization values "flexibility." For some organizations, that could mean that it's fine to wear jeans to the office, and for others you're welcome to work from home if you'd prefer. A candidate can interpret "flexibility" in many different ways. To ensure that they interpret it correctly, it's important to include multiple, different examples of the types of situations where your culture is made clear. This will not only help your candidates to see exactly what the work environment looks like but also increase the likelihood that they will understand how they should integrate into that environment.

Dual Coding[6]

Dual coding is a fancy term for a simple concept—people better understand the content if you show them visuals combined with verbal information. That is, if you want candidates to understand the work environment, the best thing you can do is show them . . . literally. In a world where we can easily do virtual interviews, the power of dual coding for understanding the culture of an organization may get missed. No longer do people stroll through and see the interactions of employees on their interview day. But if candidates can see pictures, videos, or interactive experiences where the culture of the organization is played out, they are much more likely to understand and remember those experiences.

Elaborative Interrogation[7]

There is a certain art to writing the perfect resume. And while employers can often read between the lines to interpret the quality of relevant experiences, the interview is where you get an opportunity to understand the depth behind the surface-level information contained in the resume and application. Elaborative interrogation is the process of asking how and why questions about the content that you need to understand. Perhaps a resume says that they increased sales by 50%. You might ask how they did that. Instead of just comprehending their outcome, you get a better sense of their process. Seeing that they worked at one company for many years and are now making a switch might prompt you to ask why. How and why questions therefore help you to understand how well that candidate will fit into the culture of your organization.

Knowledge Networks and Diversity

There are two key learning science-related factors that we want to share for diversity in the workplace. Both are related to the way knowledge is stored in the brain. When we see two things together over and over again, those concepts get linked in our brains, creating a network of knowledge that helps us to understand our world and make predictions.[8] The way this knowledge is stored makes a diverse workforce very important and possibly difficult to achieve.

Creativity and Innovation[9]

Diversity is critical for creativity and innovation due to our differing experiences. Here's a concrete example for you. I (Cindy) have a strong connection between the concepts of flannel and family because my dad always wears flannel shirts (it's his thing). It's unlikely that you have the same association in your brain that I have in mine. This means that if the two of us were sitting in the same marketing meeting, I would very likely interpret the content differently than you. And I would probably have different ideas (like that the ad we're working on should include some-one wearing flannel). Bringing people together who come from different backgrounds therefore creates the opportunity for ideas and innovations that otherwise wouldn't exist. Of course, this also allows us to make sure that we're considering the unique needs, backgrounds, and interests of our stakeholders.

Implicit Bias[10]

Unfortunately, the same associations that make us unique can sometimes lead us to inadvertently apply implicit biases. With limited information, we use our existing knowledge networks (which we didn't choose to create—they are based on what we have seen and heard) to make deci-sions. Because we live in a world where many of us grew up hearing and seeing negative associations with certain groups (I'm not using a concrete example here intentionally!), we can unconsciously make predictions without realizing we're doing it. These biases stem from our accumulated experiences and the societal narratives we've absorbed, often subcon-sciously influencing our expectations of others' behaviors or capabilities. Recognizing the pervasive nature of implicit biases is crucial for develop-ing hiring practices that are both equitable and inclusive.

Feedforward

It can be discouraging to candidates if they have applied and been denied roles numerous times. To make the talent sourcing process a *learning* pro-cess, consider using the principle of feedforward. Feedforward is the idea of providing feedback in a way that includes strategic action. When we look at the learning science research, individuals learn a lot more when they are given feedback than when they are not.[11] Here we use the term feedforward to indicate that the emphasis should not be on prior behav-ior (i.e., you did this right and this wrong), but rather on how that prior behavior can be shaped (i.e., you did this; next time do that).

By melding these scientific methodologies, strategic talent sourcing transforms from being merely cost-driven to becoming a value-centric process. This transition is pivotal in assembling a workforce that is not just competent but also culturally attuned to the organization, thereby fostering long-term sustainability and success.

Applying Strategic Talent Sourcing

A key dimension impacting talent acquisition is the candidate experience, influencing both the cost-effectiveness and overall success of the recruitment process. Applying learning science principles can enable organizations to optimize the recruitment process. This approach recognizes that candidates, like learners, process information and make decisions based on a variety of factors, including their perceptions, motivations, and experiences. By understanding the nuances of candidate behavior and preferences, organizations can craft approaches that resonate with applicants, enhancing their experience and streamlining the hiring process.

Candidate Motivation Example: A company faces difficulties in keeping candidates motivated and informed during the recruitment process, leading to high drop-off rates.

Solution: Implementing interactive online portals can be a highly effective solution to this challenge. These platforms allow candidates to track their application status, access FAQs, and receive updates, which helps in maintaining motivation throughout the recruitment process. For larger companies, the integration of AI-powered chatbots can provide instant responses to queries, further enhancing the candidate experience. A notable example of a company utilizing such interactive tools is the Cheesecake Factory, which successfully manages the hiring of over 40,000 employees annually while maintaining a great candidate experience.[12] For smaller organizations where a sophisticated platform or AI chatbot may not be feasible, regular personalized email updates or calls to inform candidates about their application status can provide a similar human touch to the process. For instance, a small local marketing firm might assign a team member to send personalized email updates every week to each candidate, saying something like: "We wanted to let you know that your application is currently under review by our team. We expect to move to the next stage of the recruitment process by next week." This approach, while more labor-intensive than an AI solution, ensures that candidates feel valued and informed, mirroring the engagement level that larger companies achieve through their use of interactive tools for managing large-scale hiring. This personal touch not only maintains the candidate's interest but also enhances their experience with the organization, regardless of the outcome. The key is to focus on personalized communication and utilizing multiple touchpoints such as phone calls, emails, text messages, and even social media presence to keep candidates engaged.[13] Whether through high-tech solutions or more traditional methods, maintaining candidate engagement is crucial for a successful recruitment process, and these strategies can be adapted to fit the resources and scale of any organization.

Cognitive Load Example: Candidates often experience cognitive overload during the application process, overwhelmed by complex forms, repetitive tasks, and the sheer volume of information required. This can deter potential applicants or lead to incomplete applications, reducing the pool of qualified candidates.

Solution: To mitigate this, organizations can streamline the application process by minimizing unnecessary steps and providing clear, concise instructions at each stage. For example, a technology firm could redesign its online application portal to include a progress bar, simple dropdown menus for common responses, and tooltips for tricky sections. By reducing the cognitive load, candidates can focus more on showcasing their qualifications and less on navigating the application's complexities, leading to a more efficient and candidate-friendly experience. This approach not only attracts a broader range of applicants but also enhances the company's image as an employer that values candidates' time and effort.

In the context of recruitment, simplifying the application process, providing clear and concise information, and allowing candidates to track their application status without overwhelming them with excessive details can significantly reduce cognitive load. Strategies such as writing concisely, providing scaffolding or support during the application process, and offering cognitive aids such as checklists or instructional materials can help manage cognitive load effectively. For example, implementing an online portal that offers straightforward guidance on each step of the application process, supplemented with FAQs and tips for preparing for interviews, can assist candidates in focusing on the most relevant tasks without feeling overwhelmed by the volume of information. Furthermore, giving candidates a clear roadmap of what to expect during the recruitment process helps in setting accurate expectations and enhancing the overall candidate experience. Both structured feedback sessions and personal feedback calls, along with transparent communication about the hiring process, contribute to a more positive candidate experience. For example, an e-commerce company might update its careers page to include a detailed timeline of its hiring process, from application submission to the final decision. Each stage could be described with what candidates can expect, such as: "After submitting your application, you will receive an email confirmation. Within two weeks, we'll let you know if we're moving forward with an interview." This clear communication helps set realistic expectations and reduces candidate anxiety about the unknown.

Additionally, engaging candidates in interactive tasks that mimic real job scenarios can provide practical insights into the role. For example, Forage offers virtual work experience programs that simulate real job tasks, allowing candidates to gain practical insights into roles and demonstrate their abilities in a meaningful way. This hands-on experience helps reduce the cognitive overload associated with traditional application processes by providing clear, actionable insights into potential job roles.[14] Kantar provides a comprehensive online guide for job applicants, offering detailed advice on how to apply for roles, including those not requiring a university degree, and information about their graduate schemes. Kantar's efforts to support neurodivergent candidates through additional resources and adjustments during the recruitment process exemplify a commitment to inclusive hiring practices.[15] Islington Council's application guidance aims to help candidates make a strong impression through their application forms. It offers a structured approach to completing applications, with specific advice on addressing the job description and essential criteria, thereby simplifying the process and reducing the cognitive load for applicants.[16]

Cultural Fit—Concrete Examples and Dual Coding Example: Candidates frequently encounter difficulties in fully grasping the nuances of the work environment and company culture solely through traditional job descriptions or interviews. This often leads to mismatches post-hiring and misaligned expectations. By employing a dual coding approach, where both verbal explanations and visual representations are provided, candidates can gain a more comprehensive and accurate understanding of the organizational culture. This integration helps bridge the gap between candidate expectations and the reality of the work environment, facilitating a better fit and smoother transition.

Solution: Leading corporations, including Walmart, have pioneered the use of virtual reality (VR) technology to craft immersive previews of the workplace and job roles.[17] This innovative approach enables candidates to virtually immerse themselves in their potential roles, merging visual exploration with verbal insights to deepen their understanding of the work environment and culture before committing. By facilitating a virtual "walk-through," VR experiences allow candidates to not only see but feel their place within the organization, assessing cultural fit more intuitive and aligned with dual coding principles.

This dual coding strategy strengthens candidates' connection to the organization, as they can better visualize themselves in the role and evaluate the cultural synergy. While larger corporations can develop sophisticated VR simulations, offering a rich and interactive visual-verbal narrative, smaller entities can still leverage the dual coding approach. The creation of video tours presents a viable solution. For instance, a tech startup might create a simple but engaging video tour of their office, showcasing key areas such as the workstations, communal spaces, and any unique amenities. Narration overlaid on the video could highlight the company's values, describe the team's collaborative working style, and share testimonials from current employees about why they love working there—serving the purposes of both dual coding and concrete examples of company culture. These tours, although less immersive than full VR experiences, still embody the essence of dual coding by combining visual scenes of the workplace with verbal descriptions, offering prospective candidates valuable perspectives on the working environment and what they can expect. This approach ensures that, regardless of size, organizations can effectively communicate their culture and values, enhancing the candidate's ability to gauge a fit with their personal and professional aspirations.

Culture Fit—Elaborative Interrogation Example: Traditional interview techniques often fall short in assessing a candidate's alignment with an organization's core values and work culture. This gap can lead to hiring candidates who have the skills but may not thrive in the company's specific work environment.

Solution: To address this, companies can conduct specialized culture-fit interviews. These interviews are structured to probe more deeply into how a candidate's values, behaviors, and decision-making align with the organization's core values. They typically include scenarios and questions explicitly tailored to the company's cultural aspects. For smaller companies, these culture-fit interviews might be more informal and conversational. They can focus on understanding the candidate's personality, work style, and values through open-ended questions and discussions. For instance, a local boutique advertising agency might invite a candidate to a coffee meeting for a more relaxed conversation aimed at understanding their creative philosophy and how they approach team projects: "Tell me about a time you had to adapt to a sudden change in a project's direction. How did you handle it?" This informal setting allows the candidate to share experiences and perspectives in a less pressured environment, giving insights into their adaptability and teamwork skills, which are crucial for the agency's dynamic projects. This approach allows for more personal and direct interaction, helping the interviewer gauge the candidate's fit in a more natural setting.

Larger organizations may instead opt for a more formalized interview process. This could involve structured behavioral questions, situational judgment tests, or even role-playing exercises designed to elicit responses that reveal the candidate's alignment with the company's culture. These methods allow for a more standardized and objective assessment of cultural fit across various candidates. In both cases, the key is to ensure that the questions and scenarios are reflective of the company's actual work environment and values. Many well-known companies incorporate cultural fit into their hiring processes. Google, for instance, uses a mix of structured and unstructured interviews, focusing on open-ended questions to assess alignment with their values.[18] Zappos is famous for its emphasis on cultural fit, conducting separate interviews to evaluate how a candidate's personal values match their core values.[19] Southwest Airlines' interviews include activities and questions designed to align with their values such as positivity and teamwork.[20] Netflix, renowned for its unique culture, assesses candidates based on their alignment with core values such as curiosity, risk-taking, innovation, personal growth, and integrity.[21] These examples showcase how different companies, irrespective of their size, integrate cultural fit assessments into their recruitment processes, either through formal assessments or conversational interviews, reflecting their unique company values and work environments.

Knowledge Networks and Diversity Example: Organizations must ensure that recruitment processes are equitable and inclusive, appealing to a broad spectrum of candidates.

Solution: Fostering diversity and inclusion in recruitment processes is essential to attract a wide range of candidates and create a more equitable workforce. One exemplary company that prioritizes diversity and inclusion is Microsoft. It has implemented a comprehensive approach that includes crafting inclusive job descriptions, utilizing structured interviews to reduce unconscious bias, and actively seeking diverse talent through various channels.[22] For smaller companies, community involvement initiatives can reflect their commitment to diversity and attract candidates who align with their values. For instance, a small local tech startup might partner with coding boot camps that support underrepresented groups in the tech industry, offering internships to graduates. This initiative demonstrates the startup's dedication to diversity and inclusion by directly contributing to the career development of individuals from diverse backgrounds. This practical step allows smaller companies to actively participate in diversifying the tech space, mirroring larger organizations like Microsoft's efforts but tailored to their scale and resources. Larger organizations like Microsoft leverage diverse recruiting channels, such as participating in minority-focused job fairs and utilizing specialized online platforms to source a diverse pool of candidates. These approaches not only enhance diversity but also contribute to a more innovative and inclusive work environment, ultimately benefiting the company's culture and performance.

Feedforward Example: The recruitment process can often leave candidates feeling disconnected, particularly when they do not receive feedback, understand areas for improvement, or fully grasp the hiring process. Addressing this issue can significantly enhance a company's reputation and make future hiring more efficient.

Solution: Large companies can adopt structured feedback sessions to provide candidates with insights into their performance and areas for improvement. This approach is exemplified by organizations such as Workable, which emphasize the importance of honest, detailed, and tactful feedback. They recommend practices such as telling the truth, avoiding condescension, and focusing on job-related criteria.[23] This approach not only helps rejected candidates improve but also fosters a positive perception of the company. For smaller companies, personalized feedback calls are a practical solution. These calls, while less formal than structured sessions, can still offer valuable insights in a more personal and direct manner.

For instance, a mid-sized software development company might implement a policy where every candidate receives a phone call to provide personalized feedback, highlighting strengths and areas for improvement. "We were impressed with your technical skills and the innovative solutions you proposed during the problem-solving task. For future interviews, focusing more on team collaboration examples could further showcase your fit for team-oriented roles," the HR manager might advise. This direct and constructive feedback helps candidates understand their performance and how they can improve, regardless of the outcome.

Similarly, a local retail chain could host small group sessions for candidates who reached the final interview stages but were not selected. In these sessions, they could offer general feedback on common areas for improvement observed across candidates, emphasizing that individual feedback is available on request. This approach, recommended by platforms such as Workable and SeeMeHired.com, ensures candidates receive valuable insights in a manner that is scalable for the company and beneficial for the candidates, thereby maintaining a positive image of the company and encouraging candidates to apply again in the future.[23,24]

These tailored strategies demonstrate how companies, regardless of their size, can apply learning science principles to enhance the candidate experience and make their talent sourcing more strategic and effective.

Optimized Onboarding Experience

Onboarding is more than just welcoming new hires; it's a strategic process integral to employee retention and productivity. An effective onboarding program, as noted by the Brandon Hall Group, can dramatically improve both retention and productivity.[25] This process goes beyond mere orientation, encompassing a comprehensive integration of new employees into their roles, the company's culture, expectations, and social dynamics. The success of onboarding is interconnected with the financial and cultural aspects of hiring. Poor onboarding can exacerbate costs and cultural misalignments, leading to increased turnover and financial strain. Therefore, a holistic approach is crucial, blending innovative strategies and effective methodologies to ensure the successful integration of new hires into the organizational fabric.

The integration of learning science principles into onboarding is key. They help in creating a comprehensive, engaging, and cohesive introduction to the organization, which is essential for long-term employee success and satisfaction. The following sections will delve into diverse

Figure 3.3 iStock.com/IvelinRadkov

Source: https://www.istockphoto.com/faq/using-files#illustrations-and-vectors

strategies and methods, catering to the evolving needs of talent acquisition and onboarding. We will explore high-tech and human-centric approaches, each contributing uniquely to creating an effective, engaging, and cohesive onboarding experience.

The Science Behind Optimizing Onboarding

Optimizing onboarding involves a strategic blend of learning science and psychological insights, crucial for effectively integrating new hires into an organization's culture and operations. Not only do new employees need to learn a considerable amount of knowledge and skills, but they need to be able to apply them to their positions and embed themselves in the culture. Because this is a time of rapid learning, learning science has much to offer.

Prior Knowledge[26]

When we acquire new knowledge, we build on our existing connections. This means that every person in a new situation is going to take in knowledge differently. If individuals have expertise in an area, they will learn and adapt faster than an individual who is a relative novice. This is partially due to the cognitive load associated with learning new things. If onboarding is full of technical jargon related to aspects of that industry or position, experts will readily understand the language and focus on the concepts being presented. A novice will need time to think about each word because they haven't heard them often before. Because of this, the most effective onboarding will, at a minimum, differ for individuals with different levels of expertise.

Proactive Interference[27]

Often, onboarding is designed using the firehose approach; throw everything at new employees within the first week or two and expect it all to stick. Most of us know from experience that this approach is at least ineffective, if not downright painful. Consider an onboarding process where new hires are introduced to the company through a week-long series of intensive training sessions covering everything from company policies to role-specific tasks. Initially, employees grasp the early sessions well, but as the week progresses, they struggle to retain new information, mixing up details or forgetting earlier instructions. This scenario exemplifies *proactive interference*, where the flood of information without adequate breaks hampers the ability to remember new knowledge due to the overload from previously learned material. Proactive interference can "build up" over time,[28] so the more you're trying to learn in one sitting, the worse it gets to take in new information. To mitigate this, spacing out learning with breaks and review sessions can enhance retention and understanding.

Knowledge Retention

During onboarding, new employees are inundated with crucial information, including organizational policies, company culture, role expectations, security protocols, HR procedures, and team dynamics. While this information is vital for their integration and success within the company, the sheer volume can be overwhelming. There are a few strategies that can most easily be incorporated to improve knowledge retention.

Spaced Retrieval

Above, we mentioned that learning is best when it doesn't happen in one long session. If we space out learning sessions, we can get a release from that buildup of proactive interference. But if we also review information at spaced intervals, we can substantially boost the amount that individuals remember. This can occur within a single session, a few days apart, or even a few months apart. The key is to bring important information back to mind, which reduces the rate at which it will be forgotten over time.[29] But we can make this effect even more powerful if we have learners bring the information to mind themselves. That is, instead of reviewing information, if we ask our new employees to recall it, discuss it, or use it in some way, they will be far more likely to remember that information long-term.[30] One of the best ways to have employees bring information to mind is through interactive elements such as group discussions. For example, after presenting company values, divide new employees into small groups to discuss how these values impact their daily work. This collaborative approach not only reinforces understanding but also fosters team bonding. By actively engaging with the material, employees are more likely to remember and apply what they've learned, maximizing the investment in onboarding. Learning scientists call this "retrieval practice" and it essentially means that if we want our employees to be able to retrieve information later on, we want to give them practice doing so.

Feedforward

Just a few pages ago, we discussed the importance of providing feedforward information to applicants to create a learning process and improve the quality of their applications and interviews for the future. The same concepts apply here as well. Providing constructive, actionable, and kind feedforward to new employees early and often can boost the normal learning trajectory, leading to high productivity.

Transfer of Knowledge

In addition to remembering the information received during orientation and onboarding, employees need to transfer that new knowledge to their departments and individual day-to-day roles. They need to integrate cultural norms, use newly acquired skills, and even quickly find information in the digital platforms used at the organization. In addition to some of the concepts already laid out for applicants (e.g., using concrete examples of abstract ideas), there are a few other critical strategies that can be used to promote transfer from onboarding into day-to-day organizational life.

Deliberate Practice

This idea of transfer of ideas or skills from one situation to another is notoriously difficult to achieve.[31] Humans learn in context and have a difficult time using learned information or even recognizing that they *should* use learned information when in a different situation. The best way to overcome this issue is therefore to give new employees the opportunity to practice new skills in the way they will need to use them.[32] Instead of simply showing them computer systems, put them in front of a computer and have them walk through them with you. Instead of talking about company culture, require them to engage in role-play or put them in scenarios where they can participate in that culture.

Observational Learning

Most of the concepts so far talk about learners as individuals, receiving information and applying it where needed. We haven't talked much about the other people in the room, or even the room itself. But it turns out that learning rarely occurs in isolation. We learn a considerable amount from observing the behaviors of others,[33] particularly when we view them as similar to ourselves or as role models.[34] There is also an opportunity for new employees to learn directly from others who can consider their unique needs and prior knowledge to more appropriately tailor their learning.[35]

By integrating these scientific and psychological strategies, organizations can transform the onboarding process from a basic orientation to a comprehensive, engaging, and effective integration program. This approach ensures that new employees are not only well-prepared for their roles but also deeply connected to the organizational culture and values.

Applying Optimizing Onboarding Solutions

Optimizing onboarding is a critical facet in shaping the journey of new hires, significantly impacting their integration and productivity. Grounded in learning science principles, effective onboarding transcends conventional orientation, embedding new employees not only in their roles but also within the organizational culture and dynamics. This process is key to enhancing employee retention and productivity, as highlighted by studies such as those from the Brandon Hall Group.[25] According to their findings, organizations with a strong onboarding process improve new hire retention by 82% and productivity by over 70%. As we explore the intricacies of onboarding, we will examine how innovative strategies can be tailored to address the unique needs and contexts of various organizations, ensuring a comprehensive and enriching experience for new hires. This approach is vital in aligning new employees with the ethos of the company, ensuring their seamless assimilation into the workplace.

Prior Knowledge Example: New hires often struggle with standardized onboarding processes that don't cater to their individual background knowledge.

Solution: For larger organizations, implementing adaptive, nudge-based learning platforms, similar to Deloitte's approach, can personalize the onboarding experience. For example, a large multinational corporation might use a platform that analyzes a new hire's progress through onboarding materials and automatically suggests additional, customized modules based on their engagement levels and quiz results. These platforms use predictive analytics and machine learning to customize content, enhancing engagement and retention. They adapt in real-time to each new hire's behaviors and preferences, offering a personalized onboarding journey.[36]

For smaller companies without access to such advanced technology, structured mentorship programs and peer learning groups can be effective. For instance, a small local marketing agency might assign each new hire a mentor from their department and also set up bi-weekly lunch-and-learn sessions where team members discuss various topics, from industry trends to project management tools. Pairing new hires with experienced mentors or creating small peer learning teams where new employees can share experiences and learn collectively provides a supportive and collaborative environment. This approach caters to diverse preferences without the need for high-tech solutions.

Proactive Interference Example: Due to the volume of information presented during onboarding, new employees often experience proactive interference, where early learned material hampers the retention of subsequently introduced concepts.

Solution: To tackle the challenge of proactive interference during onboarding, adopting strategies such as realistic job previews (RJP) has proved to be highly effective. This approach not only prepares new hires for the realities of their roles but also aligns their expectations with the company culture, thereby enhancing job satisfaction and reducing turnover. An article on SHRM highlights how more employers are leveraging RJPs to give applicants a clear picture of what their sought-after jobs involve. Through various formats such as face-to-face meetings, videos, and even direct participation in job tasks, RJPs offer a comprehensive insight into the day-to-day responsibilities and working conditions. This technique is particularly beneficial for roles with specific demands or unclear expectations, significantly reducing turnover rates by setting accurate job expectations from the outset.[37]

For instance, adopting strategies similar to realistic job previews (RJP) has shown significant effectiveness in improving the onboarding process. A case in point could be a tech startup that decides to tackle proactive interference by introducing an innovative onboarding approach. Recognizing that a one-size-fits-all method overwhelms new employees, they devise a plan to personalize the onboarding journey. This plan involves providing new hires with a detailed, week-long series of training sessions tailored to their specific roles and previous experiences. The sessions start with a comprehensive overview of the company culture and gradually move towards more role-specific training, incorporating interactive elements such as simulations of typical job tasks and virtual meet-and-greets with their future teams. This method aims to reduce the cognitive load by pacing the learning process and allowing new information to be assimilated more effectively.

Moreover, the startup integrates a feedback loop, inviting new hires to share their thoughts on the pacing and content of the onboarding sessions at the end of the week. This feedback is then used to refine and adjust the onboarding process for future hires, ensuring it remains responsive to individual needs and learning preferences. By customizing the onboarding experience and providing new hires with the tools to manage their learning journey, the startup not only enhances job satisfaction and retention but also sets a strong foundation for new employees to thrive.

Similarly, ADP discusses the importance of providing new hires with a realistic job preview during the recruitment process. This approach involves sharing not just the positives but also the potential challenges of the role, through short videos, virtual tours, and other media, right from the application phase. Such candidness ensures that candidates have a straightforward view of what to expect, helping to attract individuals who are better suited for the role and the organizational culture, ultimately improving employee engagement and reducing early turnover.[38]

Implementing RJPs and comprehensive onboarding preparation, as evidenced by the practices of companies discussed in SHRM and ADP, shows that when candidates are well-informed about the realities of their potential roles, organizations can significantly improve retention, engagement, and overall job satisfaction.

Spaced Retrieval Example: New hires often confront a barrage of information, leading to cognitive burden. This overload can obscure the clarity and recall of critical information introduced during onboarding.

Solution: To address the challenge of information retention during onboarding, companies can implement spaced retrieval techniques. This involves spacing out learning sessions over time and incorporating regular review sessions to reinforce key concepts.

For example, a tech startup could break down its onboarding process into shorter, more digestible modules spread out over several weeks. Additionally, they could schedule weekly review sessions where new hires revisit and practice previously learned material. This approach not only enhances retention but also promotes deeper understanding and application of knowledge, ultimately improving the effectiveness of the onboarding process and boosting employee confidence and performance. Furthermore, a small marketing agency could implement a similar approach by providing new hires with a spaced learning schedule. For example, they might divide their onboarding curriculum into modules, with each module focused on specific topics or tasks relevant to the employee's role. New hires would then engage in short, frequent learning sessions supplemented by regular review sessions to reinforce key concepts.

Real-life examples of effective onboarding practices that align with the principles of spaced retrieval offer valuable insights. For example, assigning mentors before the start date allows new hires to prepare and absorb information before formal orientation begins, effectively spacing learning over time.[39] Pipefy outlines a comprehensive approach to onboarding divided into stages, ensuring new hires gradually acclimate to the company culture and their role, which aligns with spaced learning principles by distributing learning and integration activities over a period.[40] Furthermore, practices such as completing paperwork and sharing important information before the first day, as recommended by BambooHR, can free up time for more interactive and spaced learning activities during the onboarding process.[41]

Knowledge Retention—Feedforward Example: New employees may feel uncertain about their progress and lack clear development paths. This can lead to feelings of disengagement and hinder their progress within the organization.

Solution: Regular feedback and personalized development plans are crucial elements for the effective integration and growth of new employees within an organization. This approach not only helps new hires understand their progress but also provides a clear path for their career development, aligning their personal goals with the organizational objectives. Companies including Google and IBM have implemented structured feedback mechanisms and development programs to support their employees' growth. Google, known for its innovative HR practices, emphasizes regular, constructive feedback and uses objectives and key results (OKRs) to set and communicate clear goals at all levels of the organization.[42] IBM, in contrast, offers personalized career development programs, providing resources and tools for employees to identify their strengths, set career goals, and pursue relevant learning opportunities.[43]

These companies understand that regular feedback sessions are not just about addressing areas for improvement but are also opportunities to recognize achievements and align future goals. In these sessions, employees receive constructive feedback on their work, discuss any challenges they are facing, and set goals for their personal and professional development. This ongoing dialogue ensures that employees are aligned with the organization's objectives and are actively working towards their career goals.

By implementing regular feedback and development plans, companies can enhance job satisfaction, increase engagement, and foster a culture of continuous improvement and growth. It not only helps employees in their personal development but also aligns their growth with the company's strategic goals.

Transfer of Knowledge—Deliberate Practice Example: New employees may find it challenging to connect theoretical training with real-world job scenarios.

Solution: Bridging the gap between theoretical training and practical application can be challenging for new employees. To address this, virtual reality (VR) technology offers an innovative solution. VR simulations can create realistic job scenarios and work environments, providing new hires with hands-on, interactive experiences. This approach not only familiarizes them with their future responsibilities but also actively engages them in problem-solving tasks relevant to their roles. For larger organizations with the necessary resources, such as Bosch, integrating VR into the onboarding process can be highly effective.[44] By offering immersive experiences that vividly simulate actual job scenarios, VR can enhance the connection between theoretical training and real-world application, making the onboarding process more comprehensive and engaging.

For organizations with limited resources, alternative approaches like role-playing sessions or workplace scenario workshops can be employed. For instance, a small nonprofit organization might conduct role-playing sessions where new hires, acting as project managers, navigate through a series of project planning challenges presented by their peers. "Let's simulate a scenario where you're facing unexpected budget cuts. How would you adjust your project plan to accommodate this change?" a facilitator might pose, encouraging critical thinking and application of theoretical knowledge in a practical, albeit low-tech, environment. These methods, which don't require advanced technology, can still offer interactive, practical experiences. Through these sessions, new hires can apply theoretical knowledge in simulated work situations, effectively bridging the gap between theory and practice.

In terms of real-life application, Accenture has created its own virtual onboarding room, the Nth Floor, using the Microsoft AltspaceVR platform.[45] This space allows the company to onboard large numbers of employees at once in a virtual classroom setting. Similarly, Walmart has used VR to train over 1 million employees, providing them with virtual scenarios such as Black Friday simulations to prepare them for high-stress situations.[46]

The application of VR in onboarding has shown promising results, with studies suggesting that employees trained with VR demonstrate higher recall accuracy and confidence in applying learned skills compared to traditional methods.[46] This indicates that VR can significantly enhance the onboarding process, leading to more successful employee integration and performance.

HR professionals need to consider the balance between technological advancements and maintaining the human touch in the onboarding process. While VR offers innovative solutions, it should complement, rather than replace, human interactions and traditional onboarding methods. This balanced approach ensures a more holistic and effective integration of new employees into the organization.

Transfer of Knowledge—Observational Learning Example: New hires might struggle to assimilate into the company culture or miss out on valuable knowledge from experienced colleagues.

Solution: Implementing mentorship programs can effectively address these challenges. Mentorship in the workplace can take various forms, suitable for different organizational needs and resources. Various organizations have successfully adopted different forms of mentorship, each tailored to their unique requirements:

- **One-to-One Mentoring:** This traditional method is exemplified by General Electric, which uses one-to-one mentoring for individual skill development and career progression. This approach fosters a close professional relationship between the mentor and mentee.[47]
- **Reverse Mentoring:** General Electric also pioneered reverse mentoring, where younger, tech-savvy employees mentor senior executives, particularly on internet usage and e-business strategies.[48] For instance, at General Electric, a young software engineer might mentor a senior executive on leveraging cloud computing technologies to enhance business operations. Through regular sessions, the engineer could introduce the executive to the latest cloud services, demonstrate how they can be applied to improve data management and analysis and discuss strategies for digital transformation. This approach has also been adopted by organizations such as Procter & Gamble and the Seattle Public Schools, as well as the Wharton School of Business for its MBA program.[48] For instance, at Procter & Gamble, a digital marketing specialist might guide a group of senior marketing executives through the nuances of social media marketing, illustrating how platforms such as Instagram and TikTok can be used to engage younger audiences.
- **Group Mentoring:** This can take various forms, such as facilitated group mentoring or peer group mentoring. For instance, in team group mentoring, a team works with mentors to define

mutual learning goals. The "We See The World Global Peer Mentoring Project," a collaboration between Communities in Schools of New Jersey Mentoring Success Center and Youth-Works CIC in Belfast, Northern Ireland, is an example of group mentoring involving international student interactions. In this project, students from diverse backgrounds across New Jersey and Belfast come together in virtual sessions to discuss global issues, cultural differences, and shared challenges in education and personal development. Each group, comprising students from both regions, is guided by mentors who facilitate discussions, encourage cross-cultural understanding, and help set learning objectives that are relevant to the participants' lives and aspirations. This form of group mentoring not only enhances personal growth and learning but also fosters a sense of global citizenship among participants.[48]

- **Situational Mentoring:** This type of mentoring is more focused on specific projects or challenges and is less hierarchical. It's about leveraging expertise in particular areas as needed. For example, in a tech startup, a product manager might face challenges with user interface design for a new app. Recognizing the need for specialized knowledge, the company pairs the manager with a UX/UI designer for situational mentoring. Over several weeks, the designer mentors the product manager, focusing specifically on best practices for user-centered design, conducting user research, and interpreting feedback to make informed design decisions. This approach allows the product manager to acquire specific skills relevant to the current challenge, facilitating a collaborative and flexible learning environment.

- **Peer Mentoring:** In peer mentoring, employees of equal status support and guide one another, sharing the roles of mentor and mentee. This fosters a collaborative environment and encourages knowledge sharing among peers. For instance, within a software development team, two junior developers might decide to enter into a peer mentoring relationship to enhance their coding skills and navigate the complexities of their new projects together.

They agree to meet weekly to review one another's code, share debugging tips, and discuss new programming concepts they've learned independently. This reciprocal approach to mentoring allows both participants to benefit from one another's strengths and experiences, fostering a sense of teamwork and mutual development.

For organizations with limited resources, simpler mentorship methods can be effective:

- **Structured Mentorship Programs:** Pairing new hires with experienced employees within the company for guidance and support. For example, in a structured mentorship program, a newly hired junior software developer at a tech company might be paired with a senior developer who has extensive experience in the company's primary programming languages and project management systems. The senior developer could offer regular one-on-one coding review sessions, share insights on navigating the company culture, and provide advice on career development within the tech industry.
- **Peer Learning Groups:** Creating small teams of new hires or mixed experience levels to share experiences and learn collectively. In the case of peer learning groups, a healthcare organization might organize bi-weekly meetups for new and existing nurses to discuss recent medical cases, share best practices, and explore new healthcare technologies together. These sessions could be structured around specific themes, such as patient care strategies or updates in medical regulations.

These various forms of mentorship cater to different organizational needs and resources, providing a range of options to implement effective mentoring in the workplace. Transitioning from the diverse mentorship models that cater to individual and group learning needs, it's crucial to also recognize the importance of fostering a supportive and interconnected environment for new hires. Building on foundational onboarding practices, it's essential to explore avenues that not only familiarize new hires with organizational operations but also actively engage them in the company's culture and social responsibilities. This not only amplifies the benefits of mentorship but also addresses the essential aspects of collaboration, knowledge sharing, and alignment with corporate social responsibility (CSR) initiatives. Each of these components plays a pivotal role in integrating new employees into the fabric of the company's culture and operational ethos, underscoring the multifaceted approach required for a comprehensive and effective onboarding process.

Expanding Onboarding: Beyond Basics to Engagement and Responsibility

In addition to the strategies above, we want to share some additional ideas for engaging new hires and establishing them as part of the corporate culture. The strategies below do not necessarily have direct links to learning science but can be utilized to improve the new hire experience and help them to integrate into the organization.

Collaboration and Knowledge Sharing

New hires often feel isolated and lack platforms to exchange ideas and experiences with peers. Collaboration and knowledge sharing through peer learning groups is a valuable approach adopted by various organizations to enhance the onboarding process for new hires. These groups facilitate interaction and idea exchange among employees, fostering a more inclusive and collaborative workplace culture. Deloitte, for instance, emphasizes the importance of collaborative learning and has integrated peer learning groups as part of its leadership development programs. Similarly, Bosch utilizes peer learning methods to encourage knowledge sharing and innovative thinking among its employees.[49,50]

These approaches allow new hires to connect with their colleagues, share experiences, and learn collectively, making the transition into the company smoother and more engaging. By implementing peer learning groups, organizations can provide a platform for employees to collaborate on projects, discuss challenges, and collectively find solutions, thereby enhancing their overall learning and integration experience. It's essential for organizations to structure these peer learning groups effectively to maximize their impact. Best practices include keeping the groups small, scheduling short and regular sessions, and ensuring a diverse mix of participants from different departments or functions. This diversity of perspectives can lead to richer discussions and more comprehensive learning outcomes.

Aligning New Hires with Corporate Social Responsibility (CSR)

Integrating corporate social responsibility (CSR) into the onboarding process through deliberate practice can indeed enhance the effectiveness of aligning new hires with a company's ethical and societal commitments. This approach goes beyond merely informing them about the culture and actively involves them in practices that embody the organization's values. It aligns closely with experiential learning theories, which suggest that individuals learn more effectively by doing. By participating in CSR activities from the outset, new employees can experience firsthand the impact of their company's commitment to societal issues. This method of onboarding can foster a deeper understanding and appreciation for the company's values, potentially leading to higher engagement and retention rates. This strategy not only aligns new hires with the company's ethical standards but also instills a sense of purpose and community involvement from the outset. Several companies have successfully integrated CSR into their onboarding processes. For instance, Salesforce, known for its philanthropic model, integrates CSR into every aspect of its operations, including onboarding.[51] The company encourages new employees to participate in community service and provides structured volunteering opportunities. Building off that model, companies, during the onboarding process, can have new hires introduced to the company's "1–1–1 model" of philanthropy, which dedicates 1% of the company's product, 1% of equity, and 1% of employees' time to community service.

To put this into practice, the orientation could include a scheduled day of volunteering at a local nonprofit organization, allowing new employees to engage in hands-on community service. This immediate involvement would not only showcase the company's dedication to societal issues but also embed the importance of community engagement in the minds of new employees, aligning them with the company's ethical values from the start. This approach also ensures that new hires are immediately immersed in the company's culture of giving back.

Similarly, Patagonia, a company renowned for its environmental activism, involves new hires in its environmental initiatives right from the start. Through workshops, mentoring, and active participation in environmental projects, new employees quickly become acquainted with the company's core values and commitment to sustainability.[52]

To implement CSR-focused onboarding effectively, companies can:

- Include comprehensive CSR orientation sessions to educate new hires about the company's initiatives and ways to get involved. For instance, a multinational corporation introduces a mandatory half-day CSR orientation for all new hires, during which they present their ongoing sustainability projects, partnerships with nonprofits, and employee-led environmental initiatives.
- Offer structured volunteering opportunities as part of onboarding, enabling new employees to contribute to community projects. For instance, a mid-sized software company partners with local schools to offer coding workshops. As part of their onboarding process, new employees are given the chance to lead a workshop under the company's volunteer program.
- Develop a CSR-focused mentoring program, pairing new hires with mentors actively involved in these initiatives. For instance, a retail company has a mentoring program that matches new hires with senior employees who are deeply involved in the company's CSR efforts, such as running the employee green initiative or organizing charity events.
- Encourage involvement in CSR project teams, allowing new employees to participate in planning and executing projects. For example, in a large healthcare company, new employees are encouraged to join existing CSR project teams, such as those working on improving

healthcare access in underserved communities or developing sustainable healthcare practices.

Forging Ahead with Conviction

As we synthesize the insights from our exploration of contemporary talent acquisition and onboarding strategies, it becomes clear that the integration of learning science with innovative technology is key to revolutionizing HR management. This approach, exemplified by organizations such as Deloitte, Bosch, IBM, and SAP, blends AI-powered analytics and immersive technologies with personalized, human-centric methodologies, charting a course for more efficient and impactful talent management.

The way forward in talent acquisition is guided by informed decision-making, blending technological advancement with an understanding of diverse workforce expectations. The fusion of AI, VR, and AR technologies with approaches including mentorship and community engagement reflects a cutting-edge strategy for attracting and nurturing talent. Challenges in talent acquisition transform into opportunities for growth when approached with a blend of technology and human insight. Learning science principles applied in recruitment and onboarding processes ensure alignment with the psychological needs of a modern workforce.

A commitment to continuous improvement and adaptation is essential. Organizations need to embrace new technologies while fostering a workplace culture that values personal connections and growth. This balance not only attracts top talent but fosters long-term commitment and engagement. The vision for the future is a dynamic workplace in which technology complements the human aspects of HR, turning talent management into a strategic driver of success. This holistic approach views recruitment and onboarding as parts of a continuous cycle of organizational growth and innovation.

As organizations navigate the complexities of today's talent landscape, the strategies discussed here provide a roadmap for success. Adopting these approaches positions companies to overcome current challenges and build a foundation for future resilience and competitiveness, attracting the best talent in an ever-changing world. The journey toward effective talent acquisition and onboarding is evolving, requiring a harmonious blend of innovative technology and deep human connection. The organizations that master this balance will lead the way in creating engaging and efficient workplaces for the future.

References

1   https://resources.workable.com/tutorial/faq-recruitment-budget-metrics
2   Koriat A., Bjork R. A., L., & Bar S. K. (2004). Predicting one's own forgetting: The role of experience-based and theory-based processes. *Journal of Experimental Psychology: General 133,* 643–656.
3   Bandura, A. (1994). Self-efficacy. In V. S. Ramachaudran (Ed.), *Encyclopedia of human behavior* (Vol. 4, pp. 71–81). Academic Press. (Reprinted in H. Friedman [Ed.], Encyclopedia of mental health. Academic Press, 1998.)
4   Carpenter, S. K., Cepeda, N. J., Rohrer, D., Kang, S. H., & Pashler, H. (2012). Using spacing to enhance diverse forms of learning: Review of recent research and implications for instruction. *Educational Psychology Review, 24,* 369–378.
5   Paivio, A., Walsh, M., & Bons, T. (1994). Concreteness effects on memory: When and why?. *Journal of Experimental Psychology: Learning, Memory, and Cognition, 20*(5), 1196.
6   Clark, J. M., & Paivio, A. (1987). *A dual coding perspective on encoding processes. Imagery and related mnemonic processes: Theories, individual differences, and applications* (pp. 5–33). Springer New York.
7   Pressley, M., McDaniel, M. A., Turnure, J. E., Wood, E., & Ahmad, M. (1987). Generation and precision of elaboration: Effects on intentional and incidental learning. *Journal of Experimental Psychology: Learning, Memory, and Cognition, 13*(2), 291.
8   Tsien, J. Z. (2007). The memory code. *Scientific American, 297*(1), 52–59.
9   Wang, J., Cheng, G. H. L., Chen, T., & Leung, K. (2019). Team creativity/innovation in culturally diverse teams: A meta-analysis. *Journal of Organizational Behavior, 40*(6), 693–708.
10   Greenwald, A. G., & Banaji, M. R. (1995). Implicit social cognition: Attitudes, self-esteem, and stereotypes. *Psychological Review, 102*(1), 4–27.
11   Butler, A. C., & Roediger, H. L. (2008). Feedback enhances the positive effects and reduces the negative effects of multiple-choice testing. *Memory & Cognition, 36*(3), 604–616.
12   https://www.icims.com/community/success-stories/the-cheesecake-factory/
13   https://www.trueability.com/blog/candidate-engagement/
14   https://www.theforage.com/
15   https://www.kantar.com/

16 https://www.islington.gov.uk/

17 https://www.shrm.org/topics-tools/news/technology/walmart-revolutionizes-training-virtual-reality

18 https://igotanoffer.com/blogs/tech/googleyness-leadership-interview-questions

19 https://www.zippia.com/employer/zappos-hiring-for-culture-and-the-bizarre-things-they-do/

20 https://careers.southwestair.com/hiring-process

21 https://cheshnotes.com/organizational-culture-and-cultural-values-at-netflix/

22 https://www.microsoft.com/en-us/diversity/inside-microsoft/cross-disability/hiring.aspx

23 https://resources.workable.com/stories-and-insights/giving-interview-feedback

24 https://www.seemehired.com/blog/8-best-practices-for-providing-candidate-feedback/

25 https://b2b-assets.glassdoor.com/the-true-cost-of-a-bad-hire.pdf

26 Willingham, D. T. (2006). How knowledge helps. *American Educator, 30*(1), 30–37.

27 Wixted, J. T., & Rohrer, D. (1993). Proactive interference and the dynamics of free recall. *Journal of Experimental Psychology: Learning, Memory, and Cognition, 19*(5), 1024.

28 Kliegl, O., & Bäuml, K. H. T. (2021). Buildup and release from proactive interference–Cognitive and neural mechanisms. *Neuroscience & Biobehavioral Reviews, 120,* 264–278.

29 Carpenter, S. K., Pashler, H., Wixted, J. T., & Vul, E. (2008). The effects of tests on learning and forgetting. *Memory & Cognition, 36*(2), 438–448.

30 Hopkins, R. F., Lyle, K. B., Hieb, J. L., & Ralston, P. A. (2016). Spaced retrieval practice increases college students' short-and long-term retention of mathematics knowledge. *Educational Psychology Review, 28,* 853–873.

31 Gick, M. L., & Holyoak, K. J. (1980). Analogical problem solving. *Cognitive Psychology, 12*(3), 306–355.

32 Morris, C. D., Bransford, J. D., & Franks, J. J. (1977). Levels of processing versus transfer appropriate processing. *Journal of Verbal Learning and Verbal Behavior, 16*(5), 519–533.

33 Fryling, M. J., Johnston, C., & Hayes, L. J. (2011). Understanding observational learning: An interbehavioral approach. *Analysis of Verbal Behavior, 27,* 191–203.

34 Marx, D. M., & Ko, S. J. (2012). Superstars "like" me: The effect of role model similarity on performance under threat. *European Journal of Social Psychology, 42*(7), 807–812.

35 Shabani, K., Khatib, M., & Ebadi, S. (2010). Vygotsky's zone of proximal development: Instructional implications and teachers' professional development. *English Language Teaching, 3*(4), 237–248. https://b2b-assets.glassdoor.com/the-true-cost-of-a-bad-hire.pdf

36 https://www2.deloitte.com/us/en/blog/deloitte-on-cloud-blog/2021/three-cloud-ml-approaches-for-enterprise-ai-strategy.html

37 https://www.shrm.org/topics-tools/news/hr-magazine/show-tell

38 https://www.adp.com/spark/articles/2019/08/reducing-new-hire-turnover-through-realistic-job-previews.aspx

39 https://clickup.com/blog/employee-onboarding-examples/

40 https://www.pipefy.com/blog/employee-onboarding-stages/

41 https://www.bamboohr.com/blog/10-powerful-onboarding-activities-to-try

42 https://businessmap.io/okr-resources/okr/google-okr#

43 https://www.ibm.com/blogs/ibm-training/ibms-credentials-strategy-and-its-success-factors/

44 https://www.boschservicesolutions.com/en/stories/digital-onboarding-at-bosch-service-solutions/

45 https://www.born.net/insight/vr-onboarding

46 https://resources.workable.com/stories-and-insights/vr-in-onboarding

47 https://www.mentorresources.com/mentoring-blog/bid/104810/mentoring-and-coaching-at-ge-healthcare

48 https://lindenbergergroup.com/mentoring-and-millennials-3/

49 https://www.teachfloor.com/blog/peer-to-peer-learning-workplace

50 https://www.ddiworld.com/guide/ultimate-guide-leadership-development/peer-learning-groups

51 https://www.forbes.com/sites/afdhelaziz/2022/03/01/how-salesforce-is-pioneering-a-new-model-of-citizen-philanthropy/?sh=43c5bf3a27ae

52 https://smurfitkappatransparency.ft.com/article/how-patagonia-embodying-new-kind-corporate-sustainability

4 Talent Management

Figure 4.1 iStock.com/Nuthawut Somsuk

Source: https://www.istockphoto.com/faq/using-files#illustrations-and-vectors

Venturing into the labyrinthine world of talent management, organizations find themselves in an intricate dance more complex than coordinating a flash mob in Times Square. It's a realm in which learning science plays a pivotal role, turning the traditional methods of talent management—those once as straightforward as a game of checkers—into a sophisticated game of strategic 3D Jenga.

DOI: 10.4324/9781032711591-4

In this dynamic tapestry, the principles of learning science, tailor-made for the seasoned yet ever-curious adult corporate learner, breathe new life into the talent lifecycle. At its foundation, talent management is about helping a team to reach its full potential. It's not just about filling positions but about orchestrating an ensemble in which every member plays in harmony. This chapter delves into this symphony of talent management, where acquisition, nurturing, retention, and strategic exits are conducted with the finesse of a maestro. It's a world where McKinsey's insights meet Valamis's strategies, blending into a powerful concerto of skill development and employee motivation. While talent management truly encompasses the whole of the talent cycle, here we focus on talent management as the mid-section—taking acquired talent and helping them thrive.

As we peel back the layers of this onion, we discover that talent management is not just about assigning roles and responsibilities. It's about creating a culture as nurturing as a greenhouse, where each individual flourishes. Here, employee well-being and work-life balance are not just buzzwords but the very pillars that uphold the structure. It's a journey through a landscape as dynamic and colorful as a kaleidoscope, where every turn reveals new patterns of leadership development, culture cultivation, and employee well-being, all weaving together to form a resilient and adaptive tapestry for the future.

As we delve further into the intricate world of talent management, we come across a series of enigmatic forces and mythical entities that shape its very essence. These fictional yet symbolically rich scenarios encapsulate the multifaceted challenges encountered in this realm:

The Leadership Labyrinth: In the Leadership Labyrinth, individuals enter with high hopes but soon face a convoluted path, full of dead ends and confusing turns. This maze symbolizes the complex challenge organizations face in developing future leaders. Despite recognizing the need for leadership development, many companies struggle to implement effective programs, lacking clear direction and support in leadership growth. The consequence is emerging leaders who feel lost, unprepared, and unable to reach their full potential, adversely affecting organizational growth and adaptability.

The Career Path Mirage: The Career Path Mirage represents the elusive nature of career progression within many organizations. Employees, much like travelers in a desert, seek a clear path to advancement and growth but often find these paths to be illusory. The mirage reflects the lack of transparent and defined career trajectories in the workplace. This ambiguity can erode engagement and motivation, culminating in diminished productivity. To navigate the mirage, fostering a culture of open dialogue about career aspirations and opportunities between employees and management is crucial.

The Cultural Quicksand: The Cultural Quicksand is a metaphor for the often unseen dangers lurking within an organization's culture. On the surface, everything might seem stable, but a toxic culture, poor management, and a lack of employee recognition can quickly engulf an organization's workforce, pulling them into disengagement and dissatisfaction. This scenario illustrates how crucial it is to actively foster a positive, inclusive, and supportive work environment. Neglecting this can lead to a culture where employees feel undervalued and misunderstood, increasing the risk of diminished productivity.

Recognition Echo Chamber: In the Recognition Echo Chamber, employees' efforts and achievements are echoed back unheard and unacknowledged. This space symbolizes the problem of inadequate recognition in the workplace. When employees feel that their hard work goes unnoticed, it leads to a sense of futility and disengagement. This lack of recognition can significantly impact employee morale and motivation, making them feel as though they are working in a vacuum.

Skills Mismatch Maze: The Skill Mismatch Maze is a representation of the disconnection that can occur between an employee's skills and interests and the needs of the organization. In this maze, employees find themselves either overqualified or underutilized, leading to frustration and demotivation. This mismatch can result in employees feeling trapped in roles that do not fully utilize their potential or align with their career aspirations. It highlights the importance of aligning individual skills with organizational goals to ensure job satisfaction and effectiveness.

As we navigate the intricate landscape of talent management, our exploration unveils two critical themes that shine a light through its complex challenges, enhanced by the principles of learning science: 1) leadership development and career pathing and 2) organizational culture and employee well-being. By strategically focusing on these themes and integrating learning science principles, organizations can adeptly maneuver through the challenges of talent management with greater clarity and purpose. This approach promises not just a more rewarding and enduring talent management process but also ensures the stability and growth of the workforce.

In the upcoming sections, we will dissect how these challenges manifest in the workforce and how the transformative role of learning science can convert these challenges into opportunities for organizational triumph. Mirroring the insights gained in the talent acquisition chapter, where strategic talent sourcing and optimized onboarding experience were redefined through learning science, our journey through talent management will reveal practical and innovative strategies for advancement and success. By embracing these principles, organizations can effectively tackle immediate challenges and lay a foundation for enduring resilience and prosperity.

Leadership Development and Career Pathing

Developing future leaders in talent management is a multifaceted challenge that extends beyond simply filling leadership roles. It involves nurturing the potential of future leaders to ensure the long-term success and adaptability of an organization. In spite of widespread acknowledgment

Figure 4.2 iStock.com/Viktor Morozuk
Source: https://www.istockphoto.com/faq/using-files#illustrations-and-vectors

of its importance, a stark contrast exists between recognition and action. Research from Zippia reveals a notable discrepancy: while 83% of businesses recognize the importance of investing in leadership development for entry-level roles, only about 5% have actively embarked on this transformative journey. This gap suggests a significant oversight in harnessing future leadership potential.[1,2]

Furthermore, only 48% of employees view their company's leadership as "high quality," indicating a disconnect between the perception and reality of leadership within organizations. It's as if organizations possess all the components of effective leadership but struggle to assemble them into a coherent growth path. This concern is compounded by findings from the 2023 Global Leadership Forecast by DDI, which reports a significant decline in leadership quality. The study highlights a 17% drop in leaders who believe their organizations have high-quality leadership, a figure alarmingly close to those in the aftermath of the 2007–2008 economic crisis. Such a decline points to a growing leadership crisis that could impede organizational progress and stifle innovation.[3,4,5]

Addressing this challenge isn't just about filling positions; it's about fostering a culture in which leadership development is prioritized. Effective nurturing of leadership talent is crucial for retaining employees, enhancing the skill set of the current staff, and shaping them into tomorrow's leaders. It is a cornerstone in strengthening organizational leadership, essential for sustainable growth in an ever-evolving business landscape.

The solution to this leadership development conundrum lies in the application of learning science principles. Learning science, with its insights into adult learning processes—how individuals acquire, retain, and apply knowledge and skills—provides invaluable tools for crafting effective leadership development programs. Integrating principles such as experiential learning, tailored learning pathways, and continuous feedback mechanisms, learning science can bridge the gap between potential and performance in emerging leaders.

Applying learning science to leadership development involves creating personalized growth plans that recognize individual learning trajectories and career aspirations. It also means leveraging technology and data analytics to track progress and adapt initiatives in real-time. Learning analytics can help identify skill gaps and learning preferences, enabling organizations to design targeted interventions that resonate with each leader's unique developmental needs and interests. Additionally, learning science emphasizes the importance of a growth mindset and the development of soft skills, such as emotional intelligence and adaptive thinking—skills crucial for effective leadership in dynamic business environments. By fostering these competencies, organizations can cultivate a leadership pool that is not only technically proficient but also emotionally intelligent and agile.

In essence, integrating learning science into leadership development strategies promises a more systematic, data-driven, and personalized approach. This alignment can transform the landscape of leadership development, turning the challenge of nurturing future leaders into an opportunity for building a robust, dynamic, and future-ready leadership bench.

The Science Behind Leadership Development and Career Pathing

In the quest for developing future leaders and career pathing, we encounter a landscape in which traditional approaches often fall short. This complex challenge goes beyond conventional training, calling for a nuanced strategy that aligns with modern learning science principles. The key issue lies not just in recognizing the need for leadership development but in effectively implementing a transformative journey. Many organizations, aware of its importance, still struggle to translate this awareness into actionable strategies. This gap between intent and action is where learning science provides invaluable insights.

Learning science offers a multifaceted approach to leadership development, one that recognizes the diverse needs, backgrounds, and experiences of potential leaders. It shifts the focus from a one-size-fits-all model to a more personalized, adaptive framework. This involves understanding the existing knowledge (schema) of these individuals and building on it in a way that resonates with their unique career aspirations.

Prior Knowledge and Expertise

In Chapter 3, we discussed the importance of prior knowledge for onboarding. Employees come from different backgrounds with different levels of expertise and that expertise determines the rate at which they will learn about the organization. The same is true for leadership development. New knowledge is being built on existing knowledge and therefore the foundation of existing knowledge determines the rest of the structure.[6] In addition, there is the potential for the individuals in leadership development programs to be relative experts. Some of them may know quite a bit about leadership already; some may know very little. It turns out that experts not only learn faster, but they also learn differently. Novices often need to be explicitly taught about new information, whereas experts can learn more readily through problem-solving and hands-on experience.[7] Because of these expertise effects, learning pathways that match the learner with the type of learning environment will help them develop most effectively.

Building a Feedforward Culture

We have mentioned before that feedback is extremely beneficial for learning and development of knowledge and skills.[8] Unfortunately, providing quality feedback can often be difficult both for the giver and the receiver. For feedback to be most effective, it needs to be elaborative and explanatory in nature[9] and it should be actionable, clearly telling the receiver how to move forward.[10] To maximize growth, feedback should also be frequent.[11],[12] While this might sound daunting and like it would create a negative environment, there is actually some research showing that more frequent assessments of work make people less anxious about being assessed![13] Essentially, they get used to it and they know where they stand, which makes more formal assessments less scary.

Deliberate Practice

Practice makes perfect. Just as we have discussed retrieval practice is critical for the ability to retrieve knowledge later on, any kind of skill requires practice to perfect. Deliberate practice refers to the active decision to practice, especially in situations that are challenging and therefore require learning and growth.[14] If we do the same thing, in the same situation over and over again, we get better at that one skill in that one context. But to develop stronger skills that can be used in different situations, effortful work is needed to make significant gains. In the area of leadership development, this means that emerging leaders need opportunities to practice their leadership skills in evolving situations.

Metacognition

Metacognition refers to our awareness of our knowledge.[15] How much do you know about ancient Rome? How much of this book will you remember a week from now? Answering these questions requires you to evaluate your own learning and memory and doing so accurately can help you determine areas for growth and how effectively you're achieving your goals.[16] Working on the skills of self-awareness and reflection can help emerging leaders take ownership over their own growth and help them seek out their own development opportunities.

In addition to the concepts listed above, all of the topics we talked about regarding learning during onboarding (see Chapter 3) are still relevant here as we talk about the development of leadership skills. Any kind of new information should not contain much jargon so as not to overwhelm learners.[17] We want them to focus on the content, not trying to translate fancy terms and acronyms. In addition, if we want them to retain the newly developed skills, no training should ever be one and done. They instead should get the chance to practice their new skills spaced out over time to reduce forgetting and maximize transfer to novel situations.[18],[19]

By embedding these learning science principles into leadership development programs, we can transform how future leaders are nurtured. This approach not only addresses the immediate need for effective leaders but also builds a foundation for long-term, sustainable growth in organizational leadership.

Applying Leadership Development and Career Pathing

The journey to nurture future leaders and establish clear career paths benefits immensely from the application of learning science principles. Acknowledging that potential leaders, akin to learners, are influenced by their own experiences, knowledge, and motivations, here are practical applications tailored to these unique needs.

Prior Knowledge and Expertise Example: Leadership development programs often lack customization, leading to less effective training. Deloitte, for instance, has tackled this issue through its Executive Accelerators' program, offering tailored executive leadership development experiences. This program helps senior leaders and teams with customized tools and peer groups, aiming to transform thinking and innovative leadership approaches.[20,21]

Solution: To enhance leadership capabilities effectively, organizations should consider adopting a tailored approach to leadership development. Deloitte's strategy of offering customized experiences is a prime example of how focusing on the specific needs and goals of leaders can lead to more impactful outcomes. For instance, a regional healthcare provider might implement a leadership development program that begins with an in-depth assessment of each leader's strengths, weaknesses, and career objectives. Based on the assessment results, the HR team, together with external consultants, designs a personalized development plan for each leader. For a leader aiming to improve their financial management skills, the plan might include one-on-one mentorship with the CFO, as well as enrollment in a finance for non-finance manager's workshop. "We've tailored your development plan to not only enhance your financial acumen but also to align with your goal of moving into a more strategic role within our organization," an HR specialist might explain during the plan's rollout. This customized approach ensures that leadership development is directly relevant to the individual's career path and the organization's needs, making the training more impactful and engaging for the leader.

By applying similar principles, smaller organizations can also achieve success in leadership development. Creating individualized development plans that incorporate mentorship and skill-specific workshops can align closely with each leader's career aspirations, thereby fostering a more personalized and effective development journey. For instance, consider a small tech startup that identifies a need to enhance its leadership team's capabilities in managing remote teams—a critical skill given their distributed workforce. The company decides to create individualized development plans for each of its leadership team members. For a leader who is particularly keen on improving remote team engagement, the plan might involve mentorship from an experienced executive at another company known for its exemplary remote culture.

Additionally, this leader is enrolled in a series of workshops focused on remote team dynamics, effective online communication, and digital tools for team collaboration. For example: "Based on your feedback and our growth objectives, we've partnered you with a mentor who has successfully navigated the challenges of leading remote teams. Alongside, you'll attend workshops that are selected to equip you with the skills to enhance team cohesion and productivity in a remote setting," the HR manager might convey, outlining the plan's components.

This personalized approach not only addresses the specific developmental needs of the leader but also aligns with the strategic goals of the startup to optimize remote team performance. By tailoring the development initiatives to the unique aspirations and challenges of each leader, the startup ensures that its leadership development efforts are directly relevant and maximally beneficial, thereby enhancing the overall effectiveness of its leadership team.

Building a Feedforward Culture Example: The establishment of a continuous and constructive feedback culture is crucial for leadership growth. A notable strategy in this regard is the implementation of 360° feedback, which has been widely adopted by various companies to enhance leadership development.

Solution: 360° feedback has proven to be a powerful tool for leadership development. This process involves collecting anonymous feedback from a variety of sources, including employees managed by the leader, peers, and others. This type of feedback can help an already effective manager to progress further, providing insights that enable them to step out of their comfort zone and address potential areas for improvement. For example, a director at a multinational corporation might undergo a 360° feedback session as part of an annual leadership development program.[22] This process involves gathering anonymous evaluations from their direct reports, colleagues at the same level, supervisors, and occasionally clients or other external stakeholders. The feedback might highlight strengths such as strategic thinking and team motivation, while also pointing out areas for improvement, such as the need for more effective communication with remote team members. "The insights from your team suggest a great appreciation for your visionary leadership but also indicate a desire for more frequent and direct communication on project statuses," an HR specialist might explain during the feedback review session. This comprehensive feedback allows the director to recognize the value of adopting new communication tools and techniques to better engage with remote teams, thus fostering a more inclusive and productive work environment. This example showcases how 360° feedback can be a catalyst for personal and professional growth by providing a well-rounded perspective on leadership effectiveness. While it's crucial for the feedback process to be developmental rather than punitive, it's equally important for leaders to be receptive to this feedback and use it for their growth.

Moreover, a significant number of Fortune 500 companies in the U.S. use 360° feedback to support the development of high-potential leaders. For instance, at a leading technology firm within the Fortune 500, high-potential leaders are selected annually to participate in a leadership development program that includes 360° feedback. Instead of relying on numerical scores, the program focuses on narrative feedback from a wide range of sources: direct reports, peers, supervisors, and sometimes, clients. Following the collection of feedback, a leadership coach meets with the participating leader to discuss the comments in detail. "Your team values your innovative approach to problem-solving but suggests enhancing team meetings with more open discussions to encourage diverse ideas," the coach might say, offering specific examples and strategies for improvement. This narrative approach allows the leader to understand not just what areas need development, but how to practically apply changes based on real-world examples and suggestions. It turns feedback into a roadmap for personal growth and more effective leadership, illustrating the power of detailed, narrative feedback in the development process.[23]

For smaller organizations, integrating regular feedback sessions into team meetings can effectively foster a culture of open communication and psychological safety. For example, a small startup with a team of 20 employees might dedicate the last 15 minutes of their weekly team meeting to a feedback session, where team members are encouraged to share constructive feedback with each other. The session could be structured around specific questions, such as "What's one thing we did well this week and one area where we can improve?" (You might call them glows and grows!) This approach ensures that feedback is balanced, focusing on both strengths and areas for growth. "This is a safe space to share your thoughts on how we can work better together. Remember, the goal is to help each other grow and improve," the team leader might emphasize at the beginning of each session. By normalizing the practice of giving and receiving feedback within a structured and supportive setting, the organization fosters a culture of continuous improvement and psychological safety, where team members feel valued and heard. This approach can be adapted to the organization's size and resources, ensuring continuous development and a safe environment for all team members. The key is to create a supportive atmosphere where feedback is seen as a tool for growth and development, not as a means of criticism or judgment.

Deliberate Practice Example: Real-world practice is essential in developing leadership skills, with both large and small companies employing practical project assignments in their training programs.

Solution: Various organizations have successfully incorporated on-the-job experiences and challenges into their leadership development programs. Randstad, for example, implemented a global mentoring program, providing every employee with access to mentorship and development opportunities.[24] For instance, a junior recruiter might be paired with a senior executive in a different country, allowing for a diverse exchange of knowledge and perspectives. "Through this program, you'll gain insights into global market trends, develop leadership skills, and expand your professional network," the program coordinator might explain to participants. This mentorship initiative not only facilitates personal and professional growth but also helps in embedding a culture of learning within the organization. Employees, through regular mentoring sessions, tackle real-world challenges, gain new insights, and develop a broader understanding of the business. "My mentor helped me navigate a complex client negotiation, offering strategies from their own experience. It was learning in action," a participant might share, highlighting the practical benefits of the program.

Such on-the-job learning experiences are crucial for leadership development, as they allow employees to apply theoretical knowledge in real-world scenarios, thereby enhancing their skills and confidence. The success of Randstad's global mentoring program in reducing employee turnover underscores the effectiveness of integrating practical, experiential learning opportunities into development strategies. This approach not only retains talent but also prepares the next generation of leaders by equipping them with the skills and experiences necessary to navigate the complexities of the global business environment.

Adobe also focuses on practical experiences, especially for young professionals. They offer internships and extensive educational resources, including leadership training programs, to help recent graduates transition smoothly into their roles and continue their professional growth.[25] For instance, an intern in the marketing department might be involved in real product launch campaigns, receiving guidance from senior marketers and attending workshops on digital marketing strategies and analytics. "Alongside your project work, you'll join our 'Emerging Leaders' series, where you'll learn from our executives about leadership in the digital age," an Adobe internship coordinator might explain during orientation. This holistic approach ensures that interns not only gain valuable work experience but also develop leadership skills through practical training and exposure to the company's culture of innovation. Adobe's approach to integrating educational resources, such as online courses on their Adobe Digital Academy platform, further supports the professional growth of recent graduates. "We encourage you to take courses relevant to your interests and career goals. It's an excellent way to complement your on-the-job learning," a mentor might suggest, guiding an intern to take advantage of the available resources. By offering a blend of real-world projects, leadership development, and access to educational resources, Adobe ensures that interns and recent graduates are well-prepared to meet the challenges of their professional journeys.

The Center for Creative Leadership (CCL) emphasizes the 70–20–10 framework for executive development, where 70% of learning comes from on-the-job experiences and challenges. This approach involves creating stretch assignments that put individuals in new situations, thus fostering learning and skill development.[26] For instance, a manager at a manufacturing company might be given a "stretch assignment" to lead a cross-functional team tasked with reducing production costs by 10% within 6 months. This project would require the manager to navigate unfamiliar territories, such as working closely with the finance and supply chain departments, and perhaps even negotiating with suppliers. "This assignment will not only test your problem-solving and negotiation skills but also your ability to lead a diverse team towards a common goal," a CCL-trained leadership coach might explain, highlighting the learning objectives and development opportunities within the assignment.

Such stretch assignments, as advocated by CCL, provide leaders with the practical experience necessary to develop critical skills such as strategic thinking, team leadership, and cross-functional collaboration. By placing leaders in situations where they must apply their knowledge and skills in new and challenging contexts, the 70–20–10 framework facilitates deep learning and growth, preparing them for higher levels of leadership responsibility.

These examples illustrate how companies can effectively implement practical project assignments and on-the-job learning in their leadership development programs. This approach not only enhances leadership skills but also aligns with the employees' career aspirations and the organization's strategic goals, regardless of the company's size.

Metacognition Example: Reflective leadership and metacognition are increasingly vital in leadership development, focusing on self-awareness, introspection, and continuous learning.

Solution: Harvard Business School highlights the importance of reflective leadership in business.[27] This leadership style involves regular self-examination and re-evaluation of decisions, responsibilities, and personal beliefs. It focuses on making better decisions, enhancing leadership skills, and improving team performance. For example, a leader practicing reflective leadership might end each week by reviewing key decisions made, challenges encountered, and interactions with team members. They might ask themselves, "What went well this week, and what could I have done differently? How have my actions aligned with my values and the goals of my team?" This practice encourages a mindset of continuous learning and personal growth.

Similarly, Harry M. Kraemer, a clinical professor of strategy at the Kellogg School and former CEO of Baxter International, practices and advocates for self-reflection in leadership. He has incorporated a nightly ritual of self-reflection for over 37 years, focusing on what he stands for and the kind of example he wants to set. This ritual involves asking himself critical questions such as, "Did I make decisions today that reflect my true values? How have my actions today helped or hindered my ability to lead effectively? What can I do better tomorrow?" This practice of nightly self-reflection allows Kraemer to continuously evaluate his leadership approach, ensuring it remains grounded in his values and responsive to his goals and the needs of those he leads.[28] Kraemer's disciplined approach to self-reflection illustrates the profound impact of taking stock of one's actions and decisions daily on a leader's effectiveness. It demonstrates how self-awareness, guided by core values, is instrumental in refining leadership skills, enhancing decision-making, and fostering a leadership style that is both influential and grounded in integrity.

In addition, the concept of metacognition, or "thinking about thinking," plays a crucial role in leadership development. It helps leaders improve their interpersonal skills and decision-making processes by thinking critically about their understanding of events before acting and seeking additional information when necessary. Consider a scenario in which a senior manager at a consulting firm is faced with a significant drop in team productivity. Applying the concept of metacognition, the manager takes a step back to critically analyze her initial reactions and the assumptions she's made about the causes of the productivity decline. Instead of immediately attributing the issue to a lack of effort or motivation among team members, she asks herself, "What underlying factors could be contributing to this situation? Have there been changes in the team dynamics, workload, or external pressures that I haven't fully considered?" By engaging in this "thinking about thinking," the manager realizes that recent changes in project requirements and unclear communication may have played a significant role. This insight prompts her to seek additional feedback from her team and gather more information, rather than jumping to conclusions or implementing hasty solutions. "Let's have a detailed discussion about the challenges you're facing with the current project. Your insights are crucial for us to navigate this situation effectively," she might propose in a team meeting, demonstrating an open and inquisitive leadership style.

This metacognitive approach enables the manager to discard initial negative assumptions and instead adopt a more constructive and empathetic stance toward problem-solving. As a result, she is better equipped to engage her team in open dialogue, develop trust, and collaboratively work towards resolving the conflict and making strategic adjustments to improve productivity. Through this process, not only is the immediate issue addressed more effectively, but the manager also strengthens her decision-making processes and interpersonal skills, contributing to her overall leadership development.[29]

These examples from Harvard Business School and Harry M. Kraemer, as well as the principles of metacognition, illustrate how reflective practices and self-awareness are integral to effective leadership. By incorporating these practices, leaders in various organizations can foster a more dynamic, responsive, and effective leadership style, benefiting both their personal growth and the development of their teams.

Reducing Cognitive Load in Training Example: Leadership training often overwhelms learners with complex concepts and voluminous content. This can hinder effective learning and skill application.

Solution: Microlearning is an effective solution to this challenge, as demonstrated by several companies. For instance, DDI's implementation of microlearning involves breaking down complex leadership concepts into bite-sized, easily digestible modules that leaders can explore in between their regular duties.[30] This method allows for learning to be seamlessly integrated into a leader's day-to-day routine, without overwhelming their schedule. "Our microlearning modules are designed to provide you with key insights and strategies in under 10 minutes, enabling you to apply new skills immediately," a DDI program manager might explain.

This approach has proved successful, with many organizations adopting microlearning for its efficiency and impact on skill enhancement. Google has innovatively used microlearning through "whisper courses," providing managers with actionable tips via email, leading to noticeable improvements in managerial behavior.[31] These tips are designed to be read and reflected on in moments between meetings or during a coffee break. "This week's whisper course focuses on active listening. Here's a quick exercise you can try in your next team meeting," the email might prompt, encouraging immediate application of the concept.

Freeletics and Magellan Health also employed microlearning to address training challenges, with Freeletics integrating microlearning into weekly challenges and lessons, and Magellan Health significantly increasing training participation and engagement through microlearning.[31] "This week's challenge is to identify and apply one leadership principle from our micro lesson in your interactions with your team," a Freeletics HR specialist might announce, making learning interactive and directly applicable to daily work. Magellan Health demonstrates the effectiveness of microlearning in increasing engagement and participation in training programs. By offering short, focused learning experiences, they've made it easier for employees to commit to and complete their training.

For smaller organizations, adopting microlearning strategies can be as simple as creating a series of short, focused training videos on key leadership skills or sending out weekly leadership tips via email. This approach ensures that leadership development is accessible, practical, and aligned with the time constraints and resource limitations that smaller companies often face.

Spaced Learning for Retention Example: A common challenge in leadership development programs is ensuring long-term retention of skills, with traditional methods often leading to quick forgetting of the material learned.

Solution: Spaced learning is a highly effective strategy for enhancing retention in leadership development, as discussed by various organizations and experts. This approach involves distributing learning over time rather than condensing it into a single session. For example, Culture Amp advocates for spaced repetition as a way to improve learning retention. Instead of a 2-hour workshop in one day, spaced learning breaks it down into several half-hour sessions across several days, which helps learners retain more information and apply their learning in new ways.[32] For instance, after the first half-hour session on the basics of effective communication, participants might be encouraged to apply these principles in their day-to-day interactions before the next session. "Try to use active listening in your next team meeting and reflect on the experience in our next session," a facilitator might suggest, providing a direct application of learning content. This approach not only reinforces the learning material but also encourages learners to integrate new skills into their behavior gradually. The spaced intervals between sessions allow for reflection, discussion, and application, which are crucial for deep learning. By the end of the program, participants are more likely to retain the information and incorporate these new leadership skills into their daily practices, demonstrating the power of spaced learning in enhancing learning retention and application.

WDHB, a consultancy specializing in experiential learning and leadership development, utilizes the neuroscience behind learning and memory formation, emphasizing that spaced learning works by allowing time for the material to be consolidated in the brain.[33] The method involves introducing gradually increasing intervals of time between reviewing or practicing the learned material, a concept grounded in the understanding that our brains encode information more efficiently when given the time to process and store it. For example, in a leadership development context, WDHB might design a program where participants first learn about strategic decision-making principles. Instead of immediately moving on to another topic, the program revisits the same principles after a day, then again after a week, and once more after a month. "This spacing allows your brain to consolidate what you've learned, making it easier for you to recall and apply these principles when you're faced with real-life strategic decisions," a WDHB facilitator might explain during the program. By structuring the learning experience to align with how the brain naturally processes and stores information, WDHB's programs ensure that participants not only understand the concepts but are also more likely to remember and apply them in their leadership roles, demonstrating the practical benefits of neuroscience-informed learning strategies.

Knowledge Anywhere, a provider of online training solutions, offers actionable strategies for incorporating spaced learning into corporate training programs, effectively enhancing learning retention and application.[34] Their approach includes integrating spaced learning with microlearning principles, presenting content in brief, digestible segments that are repeated over time in varied formats to maintain engagement and reinforce learning. For instance, a company might roll out a leadership development module on effective communication, initially presented as a short video. A few days later, the same concepts are reviewed through an interactive e-learning module, followed by a live webinar for discussion and application of the principles. After another interval, participants might engage in a virtual reality simulation that requires them to apply effective communication strategies in a simulated high-stress scenario. Interactive methods, such as scenario-based learning and real-world simulations, are emphasized to further solidify the learning. These methods allow participants to apply what they've learned in practical, realistic contexts, thereby enhancing their ability to recall and use the information when it matters most. Knowledge Anywhere's guidelines for spaced learning underscore the importance of variety, interactivity, and consistent reinforcement in training programs. By following these recommendations, organizations can maximize the impact of their training efforts, ensuring that employees not only learn new skills and concepts but are also able to apply them effectively in their roles.

In summary, spaced learning is not just a memory aid but also a tool for enhancing overall learning efficiency and application. It's suitable for various types of training across different industries and can be adapted to suit the specific needs of an organization, regardless of its size. This approach ensures that leadership training is both effective and manageable, aiding in the development of well-rounded leaders equipped with lasting skills.

Fostering Organizational Culture and Employee Well-being

In the realm of talent management, the essence of fostering a positive organizational culture and ensuring employee well-being shines as a beacon of utmost importance. This pivotal aspect significantly influences employee satisfaction, motivation, and retention, laying a solid foundation for a thriving work environment. Yet, the journey to cultivating such a nurturing atmosphere is fraught with challenges, prominently highlighted by the adverse effects of poor management. Research and workplace surveys have shed light on a disconcerting reality: employees subjected to subpar leadership are markedly more likely to exit their jobs in search of

Figure 4.3 iStock.com/Bohdan Skrypnyk
Source: https://www.istockphoto.com/faq/using-files#illustrations-and-vectors

better horizons. A staggering statistic reveals that a significant majority of employees have left positions due to unsatisfactory leadership, underscoring the dire need for effective management.[35]

The disconnect between recognizing the importance of leadership development and actually implementing strategies to nurture future leaders is stark. Despite the widespread acknowledgment of its critical role, only a fraction of organizations actively pursue leadership development initiatives.[2] This gap in action versus intention suggests a significant oversight in unlocking the potential of future leaders, further exacerbated by employees' dwindling confidence in their company's leadership quality.

Addressing this leadership conundrum extends beyond the mere act of filling positions; it involves a deliberate effort to foster a culture where leadership development is not just encouraged but prioritized. The application of learning science principles to this endeavor offers a beacon of hope. Insights into how adults learn, retain, and apply knowledge and skills can guide the creation of impactful leadership development programs. By integrating experiential learning, personalized learning pathways, and continuous feedback mechanisms, organizations can bridge the gap between potential and realized performance in their future leaders.

In the quest to cultivate a thriving organizational culture and promote employee well-being, leveraging learning science offers a comprehensive strategy to address the multifaceted challenges of cultural misalignments, recognition deficits, and skill mismatches. By focusing on continuous feedback, emotional intelligence, motivation, and mindset we can significantly enhance employee engagement, satisfaction, and overall productivity.

The Science Behind Fostering Organization Culture and Employee Well-being

In the ever-evolving landscape of organizational development, a growing body of research underscores the critical role of fostering an enriching organizational culture and ensuring employee well-being. This dual focus not only enhances the quality of the workplace environment but also serves as a catalyst for sustained organizational growth and success. Drawing from the interdisciplinary field of learning science, we can develop valuable pathways for organizations seeking to cultivate a culture where individuals feel valued, engaged, and aligned with their work and the broader organizational goals.

Psychological Safety[36]

Earlier in this chapter, we spoke about creating a feedforward culture. To do this effectively, though, you have to consider how feedback is landing on your team members. Constant criticism has the potential to develop into a toxic environment as opposed to one of growth. The difference between toxicity and growth? *Psychological safety.* When we feel safe, it means that we are able to take risks without fear of punishment. The team becomes a place where individuals can create and innovate, where mistakes can become opportunities for learning, and honesty becomes a priority. Creating this kind of safety doesn't have one clear strategy. Rather, consistent practices, like managers being themselves open about their mistakes and responding appropriately when their employees offer opinions, will make the difference.

Emotional Intelligence

EI is a popular term these days, but it isn't always used correctly. EI encompasses the ability to understand one's emotions and the emotions of others, self-regulate emotions, and use emotional information to guide thoughts and behaviors. There are a lot of different theories and models of emotional intelligence[37] that we won't take a deep dive into here. Instead, we focus on the important fact that EI is related to job satisfaction and ultimately to organizational effectiveness.[38] Importantly, as with many skills, EI might be more natural for some individuals than others but it can be developed over time through honest assessment and practice.[39]

Growth Mindset

Growth mindset is another term that has reached popularity in recent years, but it is also sometimes misused. Growth mindset refers to the belief that intelligence is malleable whereas a fixed mindset is the belief that intelligence is a stable trait.[40] These beliefs are shaped throughout our lives by the beliefs of those around us, the feedback we have received, and our own experiences. But having a growth mindset can lead to many positive outcomes, including higher motivation and job satisfaction, relationships, and ultimately organizational effectiveness.[41] While there have been mixed results with mindset interventions, mindset *can* change,[42] but it requires consistency and a cultural shift in the way that managers respond to their team members.

Self-determination Theory[43]

There are many different theories of motivation, but one that is used most often is self-determination theory (SDT). One nice thing about this theory is that it gives clear, actionable areas for examination and improvement. We will take a deep dive into SDT in Chapter 5, but motivation is a clear determinant of employee satisfaction and well-being that we consider here as well.

Autonomy

Autonomy refers to the subjective feeling of choice. That is, to the extent possible, individuals feel more engaged and motivated when they have choices in their work environment. These choices could include flexibility in hours or location or choice in how to tackle a problem in the workplace. The key is for individuals to recognize that there are choices rather than feeling as though their work environment and tasks are being dictated.

Competence

We all want to feel good about the work we are producing, that we're doing a good job and are capable of doing more. As our perceived productivity and success increase, so does our motivation. In order for employees to feel maximally competent, they need to be doing work that matches their unique skills. They also need to be recognized for the good work they are doing and shown that others, like them, have been successful. This last point is particularly important for new members of a team so that they have a concrete understanding of what is expected of them.

Relatedness

When individuals feel that they are cared for, their subjective well-being and, in turn, job satisfaction and productivity increase. This feeling of relatedness could stem from working toward a common goal (i.e., "we're all in it together"), or knowing that coworkers or managers care for your well-being. The critical component here is the human element or not working in isolation but as a team.

By integrating these learning science principles into the fabric of organizational culture, companies can create environments where continuous learning, emotional intelligence, personalized development, and intrinsic motivation flourish.

Applying Fostering Organization Culture and Employee Well-being

The integration of learning science principles into organizational development strategies offers a dynamic path toward enhancing workplace culture and employee well-being. Recognizing that every employee's journey within an organization is unique, and shaped by individual experiences, aspirations, and challenges, we delve into tailored applications that address these diverse needs. This approach not only enriches the employee experience but also aligns with the broader goals of fostering innovation, engagement, and a sense of belonging within the workplace, ultimately contributing to the sustainable growth and success of the organization.

Psychological Safety Example: In many organizations, traditional performance reviews often miss the mark in promoting genuine employee growth and development. Continuous feedback, embedded within a culture of psychological safety, provides a more dynamic and responsive approach. Netflix exemplifies this with its culture of daily feedback, empowering employees through open communication and decision-making autonomy.[44] This environment encourages candid discussions about performance, fostering a culture where employees feel valued and supported.

Solution: To replicate Netflix's success, companies, regardless of size, should shift towards a culture of continuous feedback. This involves training managers and employees on giving and receiving feedback effectively, thereby fostering a psychologically safe environment. For example, a FinTech startup might introduce bi-weekly one-on-one meetings between managers and their direct reports. During these meetings, both parties are encouraged to share feedback on recent projects, discuss any obstacles faced, and explore opportunities for skill development.

To emulate this in a smaller organization, the first step could involve training sessions for all employees, focusing on the principles of constructive feedback, active listening, and the importance of a growth mindset. These sessions would equip everyone with the skills needed to both give and receive feedback in a way that supports personal and professional development. These practices not only enhance employee engagement but also align individual efforts with organizational goals.[45] By institutionalizing these regular check-ins, the startup creates a routine that normalizes the exchange of feedback. This not only helps in identifying and addressing issues promptly but also in recognizing achievements and reinforcing positive behaviors. Over time, this practice builds a culture of trust and psychological safety, where employees feel valued and supported in their growth journey, mirroring the successful feedback culture at Netflix.

Emotional Intelligence and Growth Mindset Example: While specific programs targeting emotional intelligence development are not detailed, the principles behind Netflix's and Adobe's feedback cultures suggest a focus on enhancing EI across the organization. Developing emotional intelligence among employees and leaders can significantly improve communication, empathy, and conflict resolution, leading to a more cohesive and productive workplace. **Solution:** Integrating a growth mindset into the fabric of emotional intelligence (EI) development programs can amplify their impact. For example, during an EI workshop at a mid-sized software development company, the facilitator emphasizes not only recognizing and managing emotional triggers but also viewing challenges as opportunities for growth. "When we encounter difficult conversations, let's approach them as chances to enhance our empathy, communication skills, and emotional resilience. Each challenge is a step towards personal and professional growth," the facilitator might encourage. This approach aligns with the growth mindset philosophy, where feedback, even when it's critical, is seen as a valuable tool for development rather than a setback.

By encouraging employees to adopt a growth mindset, the company not only bolsters emotional intelligence but also cultivates a culture where continuous learning, resilience, and adaptability are valued. This holistic approach to development, inspired by the feedback cultures at Netflix and Adobe, ensures that the workforce is not only emotionally intelligent but also primed for ongoing improvement and innovation.

Self-Determination Theory Example: Many organizations struggle to create an environment that supports the psychological needs of autonomy, competence, and relatedness, leading to disengaged and unmotivated employees.

Solution: At Google, employee autonomy, mastery, and purpose are integral to the company's culture. Google encourages autonomy by allowing employees to work on projects they are passionate about during their "20% time," fostering a sense of competence by setting clear expectations and providing the resources needed for employees to excel in their roles, and enhancing relatedness through team-based projects and a collaborative work environment.[46] Similar to Google's approach, a small digital marketing firm might adopt a modified version of Google's "20% time" by allocating a few hours each week for employees to explore new skills or work on passion projects that could potentially benefit the company. To build competence, the firm could offer regular workshops and online courses, ensuring employees have access to the tools and knowledge they need to excel. Fostering a sense of belonging and community could involve organizing monthly team-building events and encouraging open, transparent communication across all levels of the company.

By adopting these SDT principles, even smaller organizations can create a motivating work environment where employees feel autonomous, competent, and connected, driving engagement, satisfaction, and productivity. For example, a small software development company decides to give its developers more autonomy in choosing the projects they work on. "Starting next quarter, we'll be implementing a choice-based project assignment system, allowing you to select projects that align with your interests and skills," the project manager might announce. To enhance competence, the company also introduces a "Tech Tuesdays" initiative, where employees can attend workshops or webinars on the latest technologies or development methodologies. Furthermore, to strengthen the sense of relatedness and community, the company organizes regular team-building retreats and encourages participation in cross-departmental projects. By providing more control over tasks, enhancing skill development, and fostering a strong community spirit, the company aims to create a work environment that motivates employees through autonomy, competence, and relatedness, leading to higher job satisfaction and productivity.

Adobe's transition from a traditional performance review process to a more flexible "Check-in" model demonstrates the application of adaptive learning strategies which can be used to target autonomy, competence, and relatedness. By facilitating regular, informal discussions about performance and development, Adobe has created an environment that adapts to the unique needs of each employee, promoting perceived autonomy, continuous improvement, and alignment with company goals. Organizations looking to adopt adaptive learning strategies can take inspiration from Adobe's approach by implementing regular, structured check-ins between employees and their managers. For instance, a small digital design firm, inspired by Adobe's approach to fostering a culture of continuous learning and development, decides to adopt adaptive learning strategies to enhance relatedness among its team members. To do this, the company implements a monthly "Growth and Goals" check-in using a simple online project management tool that most employees are already familiar with.

During these check-ins, each employee discusses their personal development goals, recent challenges, and achievements with their manager. To further support this individualized approach to learning and development, the firm encourages the use of an online learning platform where employees can choose courses that align with their personal and professional growth objectives. By leveraging technology for personalized learning experiences and integrating regular, structured feedback sessions, the firm not only promotes individual employee growth but also strengthens the sense of connection and support between employees and managers. This approach aligns with the relatedness component of SDT, fostering a work environment where employees feel understood, supported, and motivated to achieve their personal development goals.

By incorporating these learning science principles and practices, organizations of all sizes can create a more supportive, engaging, and effective workplace culture. These strategies emphasize the importance of continuous improvement, emotional intelligence, and personalized learning pathways in achieving organizational success and employee well-being.

Bridging Talent Management and Retention: A Forward-Looking Approach

As we look toward the future, it's clear that the path of talent management is intricately linked with the strategic retention of employees. The practices outlined in this chapter, grounded in learning science, not only aim to cultivate a vibrant organizational culture and promote employee well-being but also set the stage for a deeper exploration of talent retention. Through learning science principles, we're reminded of the pivotal role principles such as continuous feedback, psychological safety, emotional intelligence, adaptive learning, and self-determination theory play in fostering a nurturing organizational culture and promoting employee well-being. These foundations not only enhance current talent management strategies but also pave the way for effective retention, ensuring a future where organizations thrive on the resilience, engagement, and continuous growth of their workforce.

References

1 https://edainc.io/what-are-the-latest-leadership-development-trends/
2 https://www.keka.com/glossary/leadership-development
3 https://www.ddiworld.com/global-leadership-forecast-2023
4 https://www.ddiworld.com/about/media/global-leadership-forecast-2023
5 https://www.zippia.com/advice/leadership-statistics/
6 Willingham, D. T. (2006). How knowledge helps. *American Educator, 30*(1), 30–37.
7 Kalyuga, S. (2009). The expertise reversal effect. In *Managing cognitive load in adaptive multimedia learning* (pp. 58–80). IGI Global.
8 Butler, A. C., & Roediger, H. L. (2008). Feedback enhances the positive effects and reduces the negative effects of multiple-choice testing. *Memory & Cognition, 36*(3), 604–616.
9 Finn, B., Thomas, R., & Rawson, K. A. (2018). Learning more from feedback: Elaborating feedback with examples enhances concept learning. *Learning and Instruction, 54,* 104–113.
10 Cannon, M. D., & Witherspoon, R. (2005). Actionable feedback: Unlocking the power of learning and performance improvement. *Academy of Management Perspectives, 19*(2), 120–134.
11 Wulf, G., Shea, C. H., & Matschiner, S. (1998). Frequent feedback enhances complex motor skill learning. *Journal of Motor Behavior, 30*(2), 180–192.
12 Black, P., & Wiliam, D. (1998). Assessment and classroom learning. *Assessment in Education: Principles, Policy & Practice, 5*(1), 7–74.
13 Agarwal, P. K., D'antonio, L., Roediger III, H. L., McDermott, K. B., & McDaniel, M. A. (2014). Classroom-based programs of retrieval practice reduce middle school and high school students' test anxiety. *Journal of Applied Research in Memory and Cognition, 3*(3), 131–139.
14 Anders Ericsson, K. (2008). Deliberate practice and acquisition of expert performance: A general overview. *Academic Emergency Medicine, 15*(11), 988–994.
15 Metcalfe, J. (Ed.). (2013). *Metacognition.* Psychology Press.

16   Ariel, R., & Karpicke, J. D. (2018). Improving self-regulated learning with a retrieval practice intervention. *Journal of Experimental Psychology: Applied, 24*(1), 43.

17   McDonnell, L., Barker, M. K., & Wieman, C. (2016). Concepts first, jargon second improves student articulation of understanding. *Biochemistry and Molecular Biology Education, 44*(1), 12–19.

18   Rawson, K. A., & Kintsch, W. (2005). Rereading effects depend on time of test. *Journal of Educational Psychology, 97*(1), 70.

19   Morris, C. D., Bransford, J. D., & Franks, J. J. (1977). Levels of processing versus transfer appropriate processing. *Journal of Verbal Learning and Verbal Behavior, 16*(5), 519–533.

20   https://www2.deloitte.com/us/en/pages/human-capital/solutions/learning-solutions.html

21   https://www2.deloitte.com/us/en/pages/advisory/solutions/executive-develop ment-program.html

22   https://www.shrm.org/topics-tools/news/organizational-employee-develop ment/360-degree-feedback-powerful-leadership-development-tool

23   https://www.industryweek.com/leadership/corporate-culture/article/2112 1356/get-more-from-your-360

24   https://www.togetherplatform.com/blog/examples-of-leadership-development-programs

25   https://www.betterup.com/blog/companies-with-leadership-programs

26   https://www.ccl.org/articles/leading-effectively-articles/develop-strong-leaders-with-on-the-job-learning/

27   https://online.hbs.edu/blog/post/the-importance-of-reflective-leader ship-in-business

28   https://insight.kellogg.northwestern.edu/article/how-self-reflection-can-make-you-a-better-leader

29   https://projectionsinc.com/abetterleader/leadership-metacognition/

30   https://www.ddiworld.com/solutions/leadership-development/microlearning

31   https://www.zavvy.io/blog/microlearning-examples

32   https://www.cultureamp.com/blog/spaced-repetition-learning-development

33   https://wdhb.com/blog/can-you-make-learning-stick-try-spaced-learning/

34   https://www.knowledgeanywhere.com/resources/article-detail/how-to-imple ment-spaced-learning-into-your-training-program

35   https://www.completepayrollsolutions.com/blog/poor-management-in-the-workplace

36   Edmondson, A. C., & Lei, Z. (2014). Psychological safety: The history, renais sance, and future of an interpersonal construct. *Annual Review Organiza tional Psychology and Organizational Behavior, 1*(1), 23–43.

37   Hogeveen, J., Salvi, C., & Grafman, J. (2016). "Emotional Intelligence": Les sons from lesions. *Trends in Neurosciences, 39*(10), 694–705.

38 Srivastava, K. (2013). Emotional intelligence and organizational effectiveness. *Industrial Psychiatry Journal, 22*(2), 97.

39 Crowne, K. A., Young, T. M., Goldman, B., Patterson, B., Krouse, A. M., & Proenca, J. (2017). Leading nurses: Emotional intelligence and leadership development effectiveness. *Leadership in Health Services, 30*(3), 217–232.

40 Dweck, C. S. (2006). *Mindset: The new psychology of success.* Random House.

41 Han, S. J., & Stieha, V. (2020). Growth mindset for human resource development: A scoping review of the literature with recommended interventions. *Human Resource Development Review, 19*(3), 309–331.

42 Yeager, D. S., & Dweck, C. S. (2020). What can be learned from growth mindset controversies? *American Psychologist, 75*(9), 1269.

43 Deci, E. L., & Ryan, R. M. (2008). Self-determination theory: A macrotheory of human motivation, development, and health. *Canadian Psychology/Psychologie canadienne, 49*(3), 182.

44 https://thefutureorganization.com/3-pillars-of-netflixs-culture/

45 https://www.workstars.com/recognition-and-engagement-blog/2023/12/21/10-companies-with-employee-feedback-running-through-their-culture/

46 https://www.danaconnect.com/the-power-of-dedicated-innovation-time-unpacking-googles-20-time-policy/

5 Talent Retention

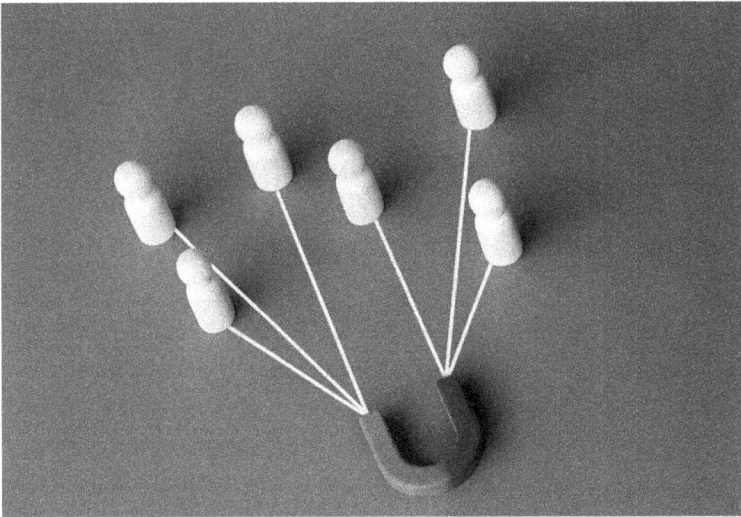

Figure 5.1 iStock.com/mohdiz zuan

Source: https://www.istockphoto.com/faq/using-files#illustrations-and-vectors

In today's fast-paced world, it's no secret that employees are seeking more than just a paycheck and an occasional pat on the back. They want it all: a harmonious work-life balance, opportunities for career growth, an inclusive environment that embraces their uniqueness, and a chance to be their true, authentic selves.

But here's the deal: organizations that fail to grasp these shifting expectations are playing a risky game of talent roulette. According to Gallup's

DOI: 10.4324/9781032711591-5

State of the Global Workplace 2023 Report, employees who are not engaged or are actively disengaged cost the world $8.8 trillion in lost productivity, which equates to 9% of global GDP. This represents an increase from the previously mentioned $7.8 trillion, highlighting the growing challenge and financial impact of employee disengagement on the global economy.[1] Losing your best employees is like misplacing your keys when you're already running late—it's frustrating, costly, and leaves you scrambling to find replacements. Quiet quitting has become a common phenomenon, where disengagement and dissatisfaction silently seep into the workplace. Employees withdraw their commitment and passion, gradually reducing productivity and stifling their true potential. Alternatively, formal quitting may occur, where individuals decide to make a more overt departure, taking their talents elsewhere in search of greener pastures.

All organizations struggle with issues of retaining their talent. Whether it is formal or quiet quitting, why does it happen in the first place? Retention is a complex issue, and it carries with it many different problems. Here are a few fictional concepts addressing real issues:

The Houdini Effect: Employees seem to vanish faster than a magician's rabbit, leaving organizations scratching their heads in bewilderment.

The Culture Clash: Often called toxic work environments, office politics can make employees feel like they're participating in their own version of a reality TV survival show.

The Learning Desert: Employees can feel stranded in a vast desert of stagnant learning opportunities leading to dissatisfaction and, ultimately, departure.

The Recognition Vacuum: Employees feel like their hard work disappears into a land far, far away. A lack of appreciation and acknowledgment can contribute to disengagement and high turnover rates.

The Mismatch Meltdown: Poor alignment between employee skills and interests and organizational needs can lead to frustration and dissatisfaction.

Stagnation Station: Nobody wants to feel trapped in a dead-end job, riding the same train to "Nowheresville" day after day. Lack of growth and advancement opportunities can leave employees feeling stagnant and unmotivated.

So how do we go about tackling these issues? We have heard more than a few times that organizations need to provide work-life balance initiatives that make employees feel like they can conquer the world and still have time for a Netflix binge. Offer growth opportunities that make them feel like they're soaring towards their goals, not stuck in a loop of monotony. And above all, create a culture that's inclusive and accepting, where everyone feels valued and respected. They need adequate pay and benefits for the work they are doing.

Are these really the solutions for the retention issue we face in organizations?

As we transition from talent management to retention, it's crucial to distinguish between developing and retaining talent. While talent management focuses on nurturing and growing employees' capabilities, retention focuses on creating an environment that encourages them to stay longer. In today's competitive landscape, employees yearn for more than compensation; they seek fulfillment, growth, and a culture that values their individuality. In bridging talent management to retention, we refine our focus from nurturing talent to strategizing their long-term stay. Gallup's research emphasizes the critical role of engagement in achieving higher profitability, lower absenteeism, lower turnover, fewer accidents at work, and higher customer loyalty. Businesses with more engaged workplaces report 23% higher profits, showcasing the significant benefits of fostering a highly engaged workforce.[2]

As we delve deeper into the intricacies of employee retention and explore the diverse challenges organizations face, it becomes clear that a comprehensive solution is needed. Work-life balance, growth opportunities, and inclusive cultures are important but these elements alone may not be enough to address the complexities of the retention puzzle. In this chapter, we delve into the dual focal points of modern organizational strategy: 1) employee engagement and 2) learning and development. By adopting a lens grounded in learning science, we aim to illuminate groundbreaking insights and leverage evidence-based practices that fundamentally transform our approach to managing the talent lifecycle. Our exploration is rooted in a deep understanding of how individuals acquire knowledge, cultivate skills, and sustain motivation over time. We dissect the complex dynamics that link continuous personal and professional growth to the enhancement of employee retention rates. Through this analysis, we reveal how fostering an environment that prioritizes learning and development not only fuels employee engagement but also secures a competitive edge by nurturing a resilient and adaptive workforce. This exploration offers a comprehensive blueprint for organizations striving to thrive in an era of rapid change and innovation, highlighting the pivotal role of integrating learning science principles into the core of talent management strategies.

Employee Engagement

Navigating talent retention is akin to untangling a complex web of ear-phones, requiring strategy, patience, and a deep understanding of what drives employee dedication and loyalty. Central to unlocking this poten-tial is a well-crafted employee engagement strategy, rooted in both the insights from learning science and bolstered by compelling statistics that underscore its importance.

Employee engagement acts as the catalyst for transforming mundane work environments into vibrant communities, where every member feels valued, understood, and motivated. It's not merely about enhancing

Figure 5.2 iStock.com/Olivier Le Moal
Source: https://www.istockphoto.com/faq/using-files#illustrations-and-vectors

productivity but about creating a culture where employees are emotionally and intellectually committed to their workplace. This commitment is demonstrated through their creativity, productivity, and overall contribution to the organization's success.

Incorporating learning science principles into engagement strategies provides a robust foundation for fostering an environment where employees thrive. For example, Gallup's research highlights the profound impact of engagement on organizational outcomes: engaged teams report 81% less absenteeism, 18% higher productivity in sales, and 23% higher profitability, showcasing the tangible benefits of a focused engagement strategy.[3] Deloitte's 2023 Global Human Capital Trends survey found that organizations with higher worker involvement in decision-making were 1.8 times more likely to have a highly engaged workforce, underscoring the significance of some of the learning science principles detailed below in enhancing engagement.[4]

In essence, employee engagement is a multifaceted strategy that, when executed thoughtfully, can lead to significant organizational benefits, including reduced turnover, increased productivity, and higher employee satisfaction. By grounding engagement efforts in the principles of learning science and adapting strategies to fit the unique context of an organization—whether large or small—leaders can cultivate an environment in which employees feel genuinely connected to their work and committed to their organization's success.

The Science Behind Employee Engagement

Many different factors impact motivation. Here we focus primarily on principles of self-determination theory, which provides actionable steps that you can analyze and implement. The best possible situation would be if each factor below could be optimally addressed, but that isn't always possible. However, if any of these are completely missing, employee motivation is likely to suffer, so make sure that each of these is adequately addressed at your organization.

Perceived Value[5]

Employees are unlikely to work hard toward a goal if they don't see the point. This is why we often see low motivation for things like annual compliance training, where the perceived value is low. Why do we have to do this *again*? Without understanding why an activity needs to happen, employees are likely to resist putting time and energy toward that task. Importantly, employees have to see the value for them and not necessarily to the organization. Maybe compliance training needs to happen because it's a federal regulation. That's important, but the employees don't really see a value-add for them. As a leader, part of your responsibility is to create value and make it transparent for the employees. For example, maybe the company will go out of business if they lose their federal funding, leaving the employees without a job. Keeping their jobs? That's value.

Self-efficacy[6]

Self-efficacy is the belief in your ability to accomplish any given task at any given time. Self-efficacy can vary from task to task (e.g., I know I can handle project management, but don't feel so great about data analytics) and from time to time (e.g., I've got a real case of the Mondays). Without high self-efficacy, motivation goes down. If an individual doesn't think there's a chance for them to succeed, they probably won't even start and certainly won't put much effort in.

Self-efficacy can be impacted in several ways:[7]

- Previous experiences. If you've succeeded at this task in the past, you're more likely to believe you can again. To pull this lever, employees should be given opportunities to feel successful (authentically; we don't want overconfidence here). This means breaking down big projects into smaller parts so that small wins can be celebrated.
- Vicarious experiences. Seeing that other people, just like you, have been successful will improve self-efficacy. But there's an important caveat here. This should not be competitive. It's not a great idea to say, "Oh look, your peer is doing awesome so you should be able to also!" because that promotes social comparison. Instead, it would be better to say, "The last person who had your job struggled a bit at first but eventually figured it out, so we're confident you'll be able to get there too."
- Positive messages. When people are told that they can succeed, they are more likely to believe it. Notably, these are messages that come before a task and not necessarily praise after task completion (although that's a good idea too!).

- Physiological/emotional state: At the end of a long day of meetings, we're not exactly excited and ready to tackle a challenging task. Similarly, if we didn't get enough sleep the night before or schedule meetings through lunch, our ability to focus and feel successful is limited. In short, employee well-being matters. Folks who are happy and have their needs met are more likely to take on a challenging task.

Relationships[8]

We are social beings and we thrive in situations in which we have a sense of belonging in the workplace. If we feel isolated we are far less likely to persist in challenging work than if we feel as though we have a team of people working toward a common goal. This isn't just about having friends (although that can help with that emotional state mentioned above). This is about feeling like you're not alone in the work that you're doing. Many jobs can be isolating, especially in today's remote work. Beyond just employee satisfaction, it is motivating for individuals to feel connected to a shared purpose, so that they don't feel alone, to increase the value of the work, and to create some social pressure not to let down the team.

Autonomy[8]

Autonomy is all about the feeling that you have some choice at work. No one wants to feel like their job is to do as they're told. Creating a sense of autonomy can be done in many ways and you do not necessarily have to give full autonomy. For example, let's go back to annual compliance training. Everyone has to do it. That doesn't feel like autonomy at all. But perhaps employees could decide when to complete the training or synchronous vs. video training. Maybe employees could choose how they display their knowledge of the content. Or maybe they could choose one of several different topics that all meet the requirements. Doing it or not isn't a choice, but giving choices about *how* to accomplish the task creates greater motivation.

Employee Recognition[9]

Employee recognition is really important. Not only does it impact that perceived value, but people are more likely to do something if they've received some reward for doing it. That said, you don't want to overdo it. The best kind of reinforcement (i.e., reward) is one that comes, on average, every X number of times you do the thing. So, if I want to make sure my employees turn in their work on time, I want to verbally praise them, maybe even publicly, every five or so times they do it. So, not literally every five . . . they should never know when the reward is coming. This is the same principle used in slot machines that makes gambling so addictive. Gotta play to win. Gotta turn in that report for a chance to please the boss.

But look out for what you reward. The best types of goals are ones that are approach-oriented rather than avoidant.[10] That is, you want to try to get something (like a bonus) and not avoid something (like getting fired or called out in a meeting). And the best goals are also mastery instead of performance-oriented.[11] "I want to get better at data analytics" is better than "I want to be recognized for my data analytic skills." Your praise should be similarly growth-oriented[12]—reward the behavior of hard work and not the hard-working nature of the person. It's a subtle difference, but it matters both for that person and the others listening. They might not be able to change their nature, but they *can* change their behavior.

You shouldn't attempt to do everything at once, but if you see that motivation is waning in your organization, you can pull one of these levers to bring it back up. All of these don't have to be maximized to motivate employees, but if you find that any of these are critically lacking, it could put motivation and engagement in jeopardy.

Applying Employee Engagement

As we embark on the exciting journey of employee engagement, let's explore practical examples of how organizations can put these strategies into action. By understanding the factors that impact engagement, organizations can craft approaches that resonate with employees on a personal level and create a vibrant work environment.

Perceived Value Example: Applying employee engagement strategies effectively requires a nuanced approach, particularly when it comes to perceived value in training programs, like harassment training. Employees may initially question the necessity of such training, expressing sentiments that they already understand professional conduct or haven't witnessed harassment firsthand. However, leaders have a pivotal role in framing these training sessions not just as a compliance exercise but as an essential component of creating a safe, inclusive, and respectful work environment.

Solution: A successful strategy, as highlighted by the U.S. Equal Employment Opportunity Commission (EEOC), involves a combination of committed leadership, accountability, comprehensive policies, accessible complaint procedures, and regular, interactive training tailored to the audience and organization. Leadership's clear, unequivocal communication about the prohibition of harassment, combined with practical, scenario-based training, helps underline the personal benefits and organizational necessity of such programs.[13]

As a leader, it is crucial to create value and make it transparent for employees, emphasizing the personal benefits and impact of harassment training. For example, leaders can highlight the importance of maintaining a safe and inclusive work environment. They can explain that harassment training not only helps prevent instances of harassment but also equips employees with knowledge and skills to identify and address inappropriate behavior, fostering a respectful and supportive workplace culture. To further emphasize the value, leaders can provide concrete examples of how harassment training empowers employees. They can explain that by completing the training, employees gain the confidence and tools to respond effectively if they ever witness or experience harassment.

Additionally, leaders can highlight the potential legal and reputational consequences for individuals and the organization if harassment occurs, underscoring the significance of prevention through training. By framing harassment training as an opportunity for personal growth, skill development, and active participation in creating a positive work environment, leaders can increase employee motivation and engagement in the training process. For example, companies such as Google and Amazon, along with other large and small organizations, have implemented varied anti-harassment training programs tailored to their specific needs and workforce dynamics.[14] These programs emphasize the importance of understanding and recognizing inappropriate behaviors, providing the tools and knowledge necessary to address and prevent harassment. By framing harassment training as not just a legal requirement but as a critical component of personal and organizational development, leaders can enhance its perceived value among employees. This approach encourages active participation and engagement in the training process, leading to a more respectful, inclusive, and productive workplace.

Self-Efficacy Example: In any organization, when an employee is tasked with a project that stretches beyond their usual scope of expertise, a series of psychological and behavioral responses can unfold, impacting both the individual and the team. Initially, the employee may grapple with a lack of confidence, feeling ill-equipped to tackle the new challenge. This uncertainty can lead to hesitation, where starting the project feels daunting, and seeking help seems like an admission of failure, further entrenching the fear of exposing their perceived inadequacy. As this apprehension grows, avoidance behavior often takes root. The employee might prioritize tasks within their comfort zone, neglecting the pressing demands of the unfamiliar project. This shift in focus, while momentarily comforting, only serves to delay the inevitable, exacerbating the issue at hand.

Solution: To address the problem of low self-efficacy and enhance motivation, the organization can implement specific strategies that build employees' belief in their abilities such as: adopting a multi-faceted approach that includes providing positive feedback, mentorship, promoting psychological safety, and goal-setting, along with nurturing employee well-being. These strategies not only boost self-confidence but also support overall performance and job satisfaction.

Incorporating systematic feedback and recognition practices, similar to those highlighted by Babbel for Business, can significantly influence employees' belief in their capabilities. Regular, positive feedback reinforces their ability to achieve set goals, thereby boosting self-efficacy.[15] For example, a manager might implement a weekly check-in meeting where they not only discuss ongoing projects but also highlight specific achievements of team members, mirroring practices similar to those highlighted by Babbel for Business. They could say, "Your innovative approach to solving the client's issue last week directly contributed to our project's success and showcases your strong problem-solving skills." This targeted feedback not only acknowledges the employee's contribution but also reinforces their confidence in their abilities.

Additionally, promoting a culture that values learning and development, as suggested by Talkdesk, offers employees the opportunity to enhance their skills through guided experience, mentoring, and role modeling, further building their self-efficacy.[16] For instance, organizations can highlight team members who initially had low expertise but managed to acquire the necessary skills and achieve positive outcomes. By showcasing these types of stories, the organization can inspire the employee and instill the belief that, with effort and support, they too can overcome their initial doubts and succeed in the project.

Mentorship plays a crucial role in providing role models for employees to emulate. Managers and leaders can act as mentors, offering guidance and support, and demonstrating self-efficacious behavior. This approach, recommended by Limeade, helps employees see successful outcomes achieved by others, making it easier for them to believe in their own success.[17] For instance, a manager at a company embracing Limeade's approach to well-being and engagement might pair a less experienced employee with a seasoned leader in a mentorship program. This mentor could share stories of their challenges and triumphs, such as how they navigated a difficult project turnaround by breaking it down into manageable tasks and systematically addressing each one.

Furthermore, managers can express their confidence in the employee's capabilities and highlight strengths, such as their creativity, critical thinking, and problem-solving skills. By consistently delivering positive messages and emphasizing the potential to excel, the employee's self-efficacy and motivation can improve.

Setting achievable goals is another critical strategy. By helping employees set and meet short-term goals, you enable them to experience mastery, which is essential for building confidence and self-efficacy. For example, a supervisor might start by assigning a new team member a small, manageable project that aligns with their current skill level. As the employee successfully completes these initial tasks, the supervisor gradually increases the complexity of assignments. This progression allows the employee to experience a series of successes, thereby reinforcing their belief in their capabilities and gradually expanding their skill set and confidence. This strategy aligns with the insights provided by Talkdesk, emphasizing the importance of aligning goals with the individual's perceived self-efficacy and gradually increasing task complexity to match their growing confidence and skills.[16]

Finally, prioritizing employee well-being and creating an environment that supports mental health, work-life balance, and a sense of safety encourages employees to take on new challenges without fear of failure. This supportive atmosphere contributes positively to their self-efficacy and overall job performance. For the employee, this could involve encouraging regular breaks, promoting stress-reduction techniques, and fostering a supportive team culture. By addressing these aspects, the employee's overall well-being and resilience can improve, enabling them to approach a project with a clearer mindset and higher motivation.

By implementing these strategies, organizations can create a supportive environment that fosters self-efficacy, enabling employees to tackle new challenges confidently, learn from their experiences, and achieve their full potential.

Relationships Example: A software developer has been working remotely for a year. Due to the nature of their work and the remote setup, they often feel isolated and disconnected from team members. They lack a sense of camaraderie and shared purpose, which results in reduced motivation to tackle complex coding projects. Without the support and social connections that come from being part of a cohesive team, their work feels less meaningful, and they struggle to find the drive to overcome challenges.

Solution: To effectively combat isolation and foster a culture of strong interpersonal connections, organizations can adopt a multi-faceted strategy that includes collaboration platforms, team-building activities, regular team meetings, mentorship and buddy systems, and recognition and celebrations, each enriched with elaborate examples:

- **Collaboration Platforms:** Collaboration platforms like Slack serve as digital hubs that streamline communication and collaboration across an organization. By centralizing project discussions, updates, and social interactions in one accessible online environment, these platforms break down geographical and departmental barriers, enabling employees to work together more efficiently and feel more connected.
- **Team-building Activities:** Team-building activities are designed to strengthen bonds between team members, improving communication, trust, and collaboration. Whether online or offline, these activities provide employees with fun and engaging opportunities to connect on a personal level, which is crucial for teams that work remotely or in different locations. For instance, to enhance camaraderie among remote teams, a tech company introduces monthly virtual escape rooms, like Puzzle Break[18] or The Escape Game.[19] Once a month, employees log into a virtual platform where they are divided into teams and tasked with solving puzzles within a set time frame. These activities not only require collaborative problem-solving and communication but also offer a fun and engaging way to learn

about one another's strengths and personalities. The excitement and camaraderie developed during these sessions carry over into daily work interactions, making teamwork more effective and enjoyable.

- **Regular Team Meetings:** Regular team meetings, whether held virtually or in person, are essential for maintaining open lines of communication and ensuring all team members are aligned with the team's goals and challenges. These meetings offer a platform for sharing updates, discussing obstacles, and celebrating achievements, fostering a sense of inclusion and community. For instance, a sales team implements weekly Zoom check-ins to foster a sense of belonging and maintain alignment on goals. During these meetings, team members discuss their weekly targets, share successful sales tactics, and brainstorm solutions to challenges. To ensure inclusivity, the team leader allocates time for a "Round Robin" segment, where each member can share one professional win and one challenge from the week, inviting advice and support from the team. This practice not only keeps the team united in their objectives but also reinforces a supportive culture where challenges are openly discussed and celebrated as opportunities for growth.

- **Mentorship and Buddy Systems:** Mentorship and buddy systems typically match individuals in the early stages of their careers with experienced professionals or colleagues, providing them with guidance, support, and a personal connection within the organization. This helps new or isolated employees integrate into the team and the company culture more smoothly, enhancing their sense of belonging. This one-on-one attention helps new employees feel welcomed and valued, accelerating their integration into the team and the organization. Through these mentorship relationships, employees receive the encouragement and advice needed to integrate smoothly into the team, ensuring no one feels isolated or unsupported.

Autonomy Example: In many organizations, employees annually undergo mandatory compliance training, which has historically been a one-size-fits-all, rigid module. This approach has led to widespread feelings of detachment and a lack of motivation among the staff, making employees feel as though they are merely ticking boxes rather than engaging in meaningful learning. They report feeling like passive participants in a process that does not recognize their unique needs. The absence of choice in how to complete the training or demonstrate understanding of the material has transformed what could be an opportunity for growth into a monotonous task.

Solution: To address the challenge of autonomy, especially in compliance training, companies can learn from engaging examples and adopt flexible working practices to empower their employees. For instance, EdApp offers compliance training courses that emphasize microlearning and interactive elements, such as "Safety in the Workplace" and "Cybersecurity & Internal Threats." These courses are designed to be digestible and engaging, allowing employees to complete training at their own pace. By dividing lessons into bite-sized key information, EdApp not only makes learning more engaging but also more flexible, allowing employees to fit training into their busy schedules without feeling overwhelmed. The use of interactive elements and gamification further enhances engagement by making learning an active rather than passive experience.[20] This approach caters to different learning preferences and schedules, allowing employees to learn at their own pace. For instance, an employee can complete a short module on identifying phishing attempts during a coffee break, applying what they've learned immediately to their daily tasks. This immediate application of knowledge reinforces learning and enhances engagement.

Moreover, companies such as Dell and Unilever have successfully implemented flexible working cultures, demonstrating how autonomy and flexibility can be integrated into various aspects of work, including training and development. Dell allows its employees to choose their working hours and work remotely, supporting them with tools like Slack and Microsoft Teams. This flexibility has led to significant savings and high employee satisfaction. For example, an employee could choose to start their day earlier or later depending on their personal commitments, using tools like Slack for communication and Microsoft Teams for collaboration, ensuring productivity remains high regardless of their location. Similarly, Unilever offers adaptable work programs and technology that enable employees to work from anywhere at any time, further endorsing the importance of trust and support from senior leaders.[21]

Personalization in training is another key strategy. Allowing employees to choose how they demonstrate their understanding can significantly increase the relevance and engagement of the training. For example, after completing a module on ethical business practices, employees could be given the option to submit a case study analysis, participate in a role-play exercise, or present their findings to their team. This flexibility caters to individual strengths, encouraging active participation and a deeper understanding of the content.

Moreover, offering a selection of training topics enables employees to engage with content that aligns with their interests or developmental needs. By providing a variety of modules, from environmental responsibility to data privacy, employees can select topics most relevant to their roles or personal growth aspirations. This approach fosters a sense of ownership over their learning journey, making compliance training more than just a mandatory task—it becomes a valuable opportunity for personal and professional development.

Encouraging employee input through feedback mechanisms like surveys or suggestion boxes is crucial for tailoring training to meet employees' needs effectively. Gathering insights after a training session can help identify what works well and what needs improvement, facilitating continuous optimization of the training content. This feedback loop ensures that training remains dynamic, responsive, and aligned with employee expectations, thereby enhancing its overall impact and efficacy.

Finally, fostering a culture of trust is essential for empowering employees and providing autonomy. This involves training managers to act as facilitators who set clear goals and provide guidelines while trusting employees to manage their responsibilities. Whether it's through flexible scheduling, remote work, or allowing employees to choose their training path, this trust-based approach promotes a sense of responsibility and engagement among employees. Managers play a pivotal role in this culture by supporting autonomy and encouraging employees to take ownership of their learning and development.

By implementing these strategies, organizations can create a more flexible, engaging, and autonomous environment for compliance training. This not only enhances the effectiveness of the training but also contributes to a positive workplace culture that values learning, development, and employee satisfaction.

Employee Recognition Example: An employee consistently goes above and beyond in their role, meeting deadlines, exceeding targets, and contributing innovative ideas to the team. However, their hard work often goes unrecognized by their manager and colleagues. This lack of employee recognition makes them feel undervalued and unmotivated, leading to decreased performance and job satisfaction.

Solutions: To cultivate a vibrant and motivated workplace, companies are increasingly adopting comprehensive recognition programs that underscore and reward outstanding performance in various innovative ways. By establishing formal recognition initiatives, organizations not only highlight exceptional achievements but also significantly boost morale and encourage continuous excellence among their workforce. For example, tech companies have been known to introduce awards like the "Innovator Award," celebrating employees who bring forward creative solutions. Such accolades often come with enticing rewards, ranging from certificates and tech gadgets to additional vacation days, thereby incentivizing ingenuity and aligning employee efforts with the company's strategic goals. Companies such as Mars, Merck, Workhuman, Full-Contact, and Paychex are celebrated for their standout employee recognition programs. These programs range from global recognition systems offering points and cash rewards, to platforms enabling peer-to-peer praise redeemable for vacations and goods.[22] Such initiatives not only acknowledge outstanding contributions but also align employee efforts with organizational values, fostering a culture of appreciation and continuous achievement.

Google has established a robust culture of recognition, implementing various programs that encourage peer-to-peer acknowledgments as well as formal awards. Google's innovative approach to employee recognition is designed to highlight and celebrate the hard work and success of its team members, reinforcing the company's commitment to appreciating and valuing employee contributions. This culture of recognition plays a significant role in maintaining high levels of employee engagement and satisfaction, making Google a benchmark for other companies aiming to foster a similar environment.[23]

Salesforce, renowned for its "Ohana Culture," emphasizes the importance of community and belonging, integrating recognition into its organizational ethos. Salesforce's approach to employee recognition is multifaceted, involving real-time acknowledgments and celebrations of achievements across the organization. This practice not only motivates employees but also promotes a sense of belonging and strengthens interpersonal relationships within teams. Salesforce's successful implementation of recognition and celebration initiatives underscores the effectiveness of such strategies in boosting morale and enhancing the overall work environment.[24]

Moreover, fostering a culture of peer recognition has proved to be a powerful tool in strengthening team bonds and enhancing the overall work environment. Platforms that enable employees to publicly acknowledge their colleagues' contributions play a crucial role in this process. For instance, a software development team could implement a "Kudos Korner" in their monthly newsletter to spotlight both individual and team achievements. Team members are encouraged to nominate colleagues who have made exceptional contributions, with each nomination accompanied by a brief story explaining the achievement. Winners might receive small tokens of appreciation, such as gift cards or extra time off. This initiative, inspired by practices at companies including Google and Salesforce, not only highlights individual and team successes but also cultivates a culture of recognition and motivation, reinforcing the team's collective identity and spirit. Platforms like Matter allow for seamless integration of recognition programs within tools like Slack or Microsoft Teams, enabling employees to send kudos and constructive feedback, thus promoting a culture of appreciation and collaboration. Companies successfully implementing these strategies, such as Mars with its Make the Difference Awards and Merck with its global INSPIRE program, highlight the power of acknowledging team members' contributions to foster a positive and engaged workplace.[22,25] Celebrating these achievements publicly not only motivates employees but also strengthens interpersonal relationships within the team, contributing to a positive and engaging work environment.

In addition, aligning recognition with the organization's overarching goals and values further ensures that employees' contributions are not only acknowledged but also resonate with the company's mission. This alignment is crucial for reinforcing the connection between individual efforts and broader organizational success. Companies can achieve this by clearly defining their mission, vision, and values, and then connecting employees' roles and achievements with these elements. Tools like goal alignment software help visualize organizational structure and clarify how individual contributions support broader business objectives. This approach not only motivates employees by linking their work to the company's success but also fosters a unified culture driven by shared goals and values. Nonprofit organizations, for instance, have been known to spotlight employees who embody core values such as compassion and innovation, sharing their stories to inspire others and underscore the importance of values-aligned behavior.[26]

Striking the right balance in recognition frequency is also key to maintaining engagement and motivation. By interspersing regular acknowledgments with unexpected moments of recognition, companies can keep employees eagerly anticipating potential accolades, thus driving ongoing performance excellence. For example, marketing firms could unexpectedly commend team members for their contributions, introducing a layer of surprise that heightens engagement and drives superior performance.

Lastly, emphasizing growth and mastery by recognizing employees' dedication to personal and professional development fosters a culture of continuous learning. Consulting firms, for example, might establish recognition systems like a "Learning Leaderboard" to celebrate those who pursue further education and skill development. This not only acknowledges individual growth efforts but also promotes a learning-oriented culture within the organization.

By adopting these strategies, organizations can significantly boost employee motivation and engagement through a comprehensive and thoughtful recognition program. Regular, meaningful recognition goes beyond merely enhancing morale; it actively reinforces the behaviors and attitudes that contribute to the success of both individuals and the organization as a whole. It ensures that employees' efforts are aligned with organizational goals, thereby fostering a positive and productive work environment. Such an environment is conducive to continuous growth and success, as it encourages employees to strive for excellence and innovation.

Learning and Development

Growth and retention go beyond mere buzzwords; they are the driving forces that propel organizations to new heights. By prioritizing learning and development (L&D), a world of boundless possibilities opens up,

Figure 5.3 iStock.com/tadamichi
Source: https://www.istockphoto.com/faq/using-files#illustrations-and-vectors

leading to remarkable organizational growth and the retention of top talent. Let's explore the advantages of focusing on L&D and how it can pave the way for success:

- Attracting Top Talent. Cultivating a culture of continuous learning turns your organization into a magnet for exceptional employees. For example, offering robust L&D programs that provide opportunities for skill development and career growth will attract highly skilled professionals seeking personal and professional advancement.
- Boosting Competitiveness. Embracing L&D transforms your organization into a powerhouse of innovation and agility. By fostering a learning environment in which employees are encouraged to develop new ideas and stay updated with industry trends, you can surpass rivals and position your organization at the forefront of your industry.
- Fostering Productivity and Efficiency. Investing in L&D empowers your employees with the tools and knowledge needed to excel. By equipping your employees with the right skills and knowledge, you position your organization to seize growth opportunities at every turn. For instance, providing training programs on time management and productivity techniques or offering specialized training in emerging

technologies or market trends enables your organization to capital-
ize on industry shifts and stay ahead of the curve. This further equips
employees with essential skills to streamline their work processes,
resulting in increased productivity and improved organizational
performance.

- Igniting Employee Engagement and Morale. L&D nurtures a sense
of purpose and fulfillment among your workforce. Encouraging
employees to participate in skill development workshops, mentorship programs, or leadership training fosters a culture of growth and
engagement, leading to higher employee satisfaction and a positive
work environment.

Recognizing the immense value of L&D, it's essential to leverage the
power of learning science to effectively address these opportunities. By
doing so, you unlock the vast potential within your organization, creating a thriving ecosystem where growth, success, and fulfillment reign
supreme.

The Science Behind Learning and Development

Our focus for learning and development is on three factors that impact the
ability of employees to remember and use anything from L&D sessions.
No organization wants to waste time and money and no employee wants
to be forced to sit through a training that is meaningless to them. L&D
therefore has the opportunity to create a motivated team of employees
who are at the cutting edge of the field or burn them out and take company dollars with them.

Different Learners

One area where learning and development sometimes fall flat is in providing the same training to every individual. Instead, employers need to
consider the varying goals of their employees. Some may want to be at
the cutting edge of their field and interested in the latest technologies.
Some may want to shift to a new line of work and would like development options outside of their current role. Some may be hoping for
advancement and interested in leadership training. The key is that one
size does not fit all when it comes to L&D. To hit that perceived value and

autonomy that we talked about for engagement, employees need to be given options that fit their needs.

But it's not just about their needs; background matters too.[27] Have you ever sat in a highly technical meeting and been unable to follow along because you didn't understand half the words? Have you ever read something dense and found yourself looking up definitions? As discussed in Chapter 3, individuals who are experts in an area tend to forget what it was like to be new. When it comes to L&D the same is true. Employees who are new to an area or a company need a different kind of training than those who have been working in their role for 15 years. The rookies might need "Intro to AI" while the veterans might want "Current trends in AI". The language, content, and even delivery should differ. Novices need more direct instruction, while experts are more likely to benefit from strategic thinking activities as part of their learning experience.[28]

Transfer of Training

For any kind of learning to be effective, learners need to be able to use information in a meaningful way. The strategy for the application depends on whether there is a specific place where you know the information will be used or if it is more generally applied.

But, we have some bad news. Humans are terrible at applying information.[29] Even with the best intentions, getting folks to take information from training and use it at their desks is a challenge. One of the best ways to help them make this leap is to reduce or get rid of the leap altogether. That means that employees should be given the opportunity to practice new skills during the training, in the same way that they will need to when they get back to work.[30] Participants can bring work with them to apply during the session or you can set up role-play activities (I know, people tend to hate things that are good for them). You can also design activities that mimic real-world applications.

Not every training session can involve lots of activities. But, during any kind of L&D session, learners need concrete examples of ideas that are presented. People tend to do this quite naturally. For example, at the beginning of this chapter, we told you that we were talking about retention (an abstract idea), but then we defined it by giving you examples of retention problems. Using concrete examples is a great way to help learners recognize where they can use the information they're learning.[31] But concrete examples aren't always used most effectively. If we want our learners to be able to apply to new situations, we need to give them numerous varied examples. One example is good, but it only shows people how to apply it to that situation. If you show them the many ways they can use the concept, they are more likely to recognize others out in the world.[32]

Maintenance

Ok, so we've created meaningful training sessions that will motivate our employees. They can see how useful they are and they're excited to try out their new skills. How do we make sure that actually happens? How can we make sure they've remembered anything and that we haven't wasted time and money? Again, learning science has a lot to say, but we are going to focus on one very impactful strategy that can help your employees remember information in the long term. That strategy is *spaced retrieval*.[33]

Spaced retrieval is exactly what it sounds like. Individuals retrieve the information they learned, spaced out over time. This means that no L&D should be one-and-done. Rather, individuals should be given opportunities to re-engage with that material at various time points. Ideally, employees will be given an opportunity to recall what they learned at each re-engagement. For example, say a training happened at the beginning of March. At the beginning of April, in the all-hands meeting, folks would be split into groups to recall as much as they could from the March meeting and to apply it to solve a problem. Then groups could come back together to fill in the gaps. This could be done again 6 months later, etc. The goal would be to have a set time for spaced retrieval of anything employees learned that you want them to continue to use. This is especially important for those concepts that are not used in daily work and may require reminders to be maintained.

Applications of Learning and Development

In our exploration of learning science and its impact on learning and development, we've uncovered strategies and techniques that can revolutionize how organizations approach employee growth and skill enhancement. But how can we turn these concepts into practical solutions that address L&D challenges?

Different Learners Example: An organization invests in a new learning and development program to enhance the skills and knowledge of its employees. However, the program fails to engage and deliver meaningful results because it takes a one-size-fits-all approach.

Solution: To effectively cater to diverse learning needs within an organization, adopting a multifaceted approach to L&D is essential. This strategy involves creating personalized learning paths tailored to individual employee goals and aspirations, offering a variety of training options from technical skills to leadership development. For instance, a software company might implement personalized learning paths by assessing individual employee skills and career goals to tailor training programs accordingly. This could involve offering a variety of courses ranging from advanced programming languages for developers looking to enhance their technical expertise, to leadership and management courses for those aspiring to transition into managerial roles. This approach ensures that employees receive relevant, engaging training that aligns with their personal development goals and the company's strategic objectives, leading to increased motivation and job satisfaction. For example, Air Methods transformed its pilot training through AI-driven personalized learning, significantly cutting training duration and enhancing efficiency. This innovative approach tailors training content to match each pilot's specific needs and knowledge level, optimizing learning outcomes. By focusing on relevance and personalization, Air Methods ensures that training is directly aligned with pilots' career goals and operational requirements, leading to increased engagement and motivation among its workforce.[34]

Additionally, differentiating content and delivery ensures that training is relevant for all levels of expertise, from novices to seasoned professionals. Acknowledge that employees have different levels of expertise and experience. Tailor the content, language, and delivery of training programs to cater to the needs of both novices and experts. For newcomers or those transitioning to new roles, offer foundational or introductory training that provides clear and direct instruction. For seasoned professionals, offer advanced or specialized training that includes strategic thinking activities and promotes deeper understanding and application of knowledge. For example, in a healthcare organization, foundational training for new nurses might include basic patient care techniques, while advanced training for experienced nurses could involve specialized courses in critical care, leadership in nursing, or research methods. This ensures that every nurse, regardless of their experience level, receives training that is not only relevant but also conducive to their professional growth and the organization's goals.

Lastly, combine different learning modalities and formats, such as in-person workshops, online courses, webinars, mentoring, and on-the-job training. By utilizing a blend of approaches, organizations can accommodate different learning preferences, ensuring that employees have access to the most effective and engaging learning experiences. For instance, a company might implement blended learning by combining online courses for theoretical knowledge with in-person workshops for practical skills application, supplemented by webinars for updates on industry trends. Mentoring pairs less experienced employees with veterans for personalized guidance, while on-the-job training offers real-world experience. This holistic approach ensures all employees benefit from a comprehensive and engaging development program.

Transfer of Training Example: A company is providing training on effective communication skills to its employees. The training aims to equip employees with the necessary skills to communicate effectively within their current roles and also to develop transferable skills that can be used in future positions.

Solution: To address this challenge, two specific approaches can be implemented. First, during the training session, participants should be given ample opportunities to practice the newly acquired communication skills. This can be achieved by incorporating

practical exercises and activities that simulate real workplace scenarios. Participants can bring their actual work-related challenges
to the training session, allowing them to directly apply the learned
skills in a meaningful way. Role-playing activities can also be utilized to simulate interpersonal interactions and provide a safe space
for employees to practice their communication skills. Second,
when introducing new concepts or skills in training programs, it's
crucial to anchor the learning in reality by providing learners with a
range of concrete examples that illustrate the practical application
of these skills across diverse situations. This method transcends the
limitations of single-example learning, opening up a panorama of
possibilities for the application of new skills. For instance, in a communication skills workshop, instead of solely discussing the importance of active listening in team meetings, facilitators could offer
varied examples including client negotiations, conflict resolution
with colleagues, and providing constructive feedback during performance reviews. This multifaceted approach recognizes the pivotal role of communication training in corporate settings and aligns
with the need for tailored, practice-oriented training that addresses
specific workplace challenges and enhances overall communication proficiency.[35]

Each example above serves to illuminate the multifaceted nature
of communication skills, highlighting their relevance in different
workplace scenarios from managerial discussions to customer
service interactions. This approach not only enriches the learning
experience but also empowers learners to adapt and apply their
skills fluidly across myriad situations they will inevitably face in
their professional lives, thus fostering a deeper and more versatile
understanding of the material.

Maintenance Example: A company conducts a training session on a
new software system for its employees. The training is comprehensive and engaging, and employees are excited to implement their

newfound knowledge. However, as time passes, employees may start forgetting certain aspects of the training, leading to underutilization of the software and decreased efficiency.

Solution: To enhance information retention post-training, integrating a spaced retrieval strategy with structured sessions—like the "present, recall, understand" model—can be highly effective. For instance, a tech company could implement this by first presenting a classroom lecture on cybersecurity principles (present), then conducting a follow-up session with quizzes on key protocols (recall), and, finally, organizing a workshop where employees apply their knowledge to simulated hacking scenarios (understand). This structured approach ensures knowledge is not only remembered but effectively applied in the workplace, significantly boosting long-term retention and integration into daily tasks.[36] To solidify training outcomes, scheduling periodic reinforcement sessions—such as 6 months or annually after initial training—can be highly effective. These sessions, blending individual and group activities, ensure active engagement and help employees refresh their understanding of the content. This strategy not only strengthens memory but also reinforces the practical application of learned skills, making the training more impactful and enduring in the long term. For example, a finance firm might hold a half-day workshop 6 months after initial risk management training, where employees engage in scenario-based exercises to apply risk assessment techniques. This could involve analyzing case studies in small groups, followed by individual simulations that challenge them to identify and mitigate potential financial risks. This periodic reinforcement ensures that employees not only recall the training material but also deepen their understanding through practical application, making the skills more ingrained and readily accessible in their daily work.

Integrating strategies like spaced repetition and retrieval into L&D programs can dramatically improve knowledge retention and practical application in the workplace. This ensures training investments yield long-lasting benefits, countering the natural tendency to forget. Just as a well-stocked dessert table entices the hungry, a positive work environment retains talent. Creating a workplace that continuously offers growth and satisfaction guarantees the enduring success and happiness of employees.

Talent Retention to Talent Exits: Navigating the Talent Lifecycle

As we conclude our exploration of employee retention, it's clear that the stakes are higher than ever in today's dynamic work environment. Employees seek more than mere financial rewards; they yearn for a workplace that offers growth, fulfillment, and an acknowledgment of their uniqueness. Organizations that overlook these evolving needs risk significant losses, not only in productivity but also in the invaluable human talent that drives innovation and growth. The solution lies in a strategic approach that goes beyond traditional retention tactics. By fostering an environment that emphasizes continuous learning, engagement, and development, companies can create a vibrant culture that not only attracts top talent but also inspires them to stay.

References

1 https://www.gallup.com/workplace/393497/world-trillion-workplace-prob lem.aspx
2 https://www.unleash.ai/employee-experience-and-engagement/ gallup-low-engagement-costs-the-economy-7-8trn/
3 https://www.yourthoughtpartner.com/blog/employee-engagement-statistics
4 https://www2.deloitte.com/us/en/insights/focus/human-capital-trends. html#read-the-introduction
5 Hulleman, C. S., Durik, A. M., Schweigert, S. A., & Harackiewicz, J. M. (2008). Task values, achievement goals, and interest: An integrative analysis. *Journal of Educational Psychology, 100*(2), 398.
6 Pintrich, P., & Schunk, D. (2002). *Motivation in education: Theory research and applications.* Merrill Prentice-Hall.
7 Bandura, A. (1994). Self-efficacy. In V. S. Ramachaudran (Ed.), *Encyclopedia of human behavior* (Vol. 4, pp. 71–81). Academic Press. (Reprinted in H. Friedman [Ed.], *Encyclopedia of mental health.* Academic Press, 1998.)

8   Deci, E. L., & Ryan, R. M. (2008). Self-determination theory: A macrotheory of human motivation, development, and health. *Canadian Psychology/Psychologie canadienne, 49*(3), 182.

9   Skinner, B. F. (1958). Reinforcement today. *American Psychologist, 13*(3), 94.

10 Elliot, A. J., & Sheldon, K. M. (1997). Avoidance achievement motivation: A personal goals analysis. *Journal of Personality and Social Psychology, 73*(1), 171.

11 Linnenbrink, E. A., & Pintrich, P. R. (2002). The role of motivational beliefs in conceptual change. *Reconsidering Conceptual Change: Issues in Theory and Practice,* 115–135.

12 Dweck, C. S. (1999). *Self-theories: Their role in motivation, personality, and development.* Taylor & Francis/Psychology Press.

13 https://www.eeoc.gov/laws/guidance/promising-practices-preventing-harassment

14 https://www.getimpactly.com/resources/how-to-implement-an-effective-anti-harassment-training-plan

15 https://www.babbelforbusiness.com/us/blog/self-efficacy/

16 https://www.talkdesk.com/blog/9-tips-increase-self-efficacy-in-the-workplace/

17 https://www.limeade.com/resources/blog/tips-to-increase-self-efficacy-in-the-workplace/

18 https://teambuilding.com/blog/virtual-escape-rooms

19 https://theescapegame.com/remote-adventures/

20 https://www.edapp.com/course-collection/compliance-training-examples/

21 https://www.insightsforprofessionals.com/hr/pay-and-benefits/companies-nailed-flexible-working

22 https://builtin.com/employee-engagement/companies-with-the-best-employee-recognition-programs

23 https://nxlperformance.com/resource/employee-recognition-programs-perks-google/

24 https://www.workato.com/the-connector/salesforce-ohana-community-building/

25 https://matterapp.com/blog/peer-recognition-program

26 https://www.betterworks.com/magazine/how-to-align-employees-with-company-values/

27 Willingham, D. T. (2006). How knowledge helps. *American Educator, 30*(1), 30–37.

28 Kalyuga, S., Chandler, P., & Sweller, J. (1998). Levels of expertise and instructional design. *Human factors, 40*(1), 1–17.

29 Gick, M. L., & Holyoak, K. J. (1980). Analogical problem solving. *Cognitive Psychology, 12*(3), 306–355.

30 Morris, C. D., Bransford, J. D., & Franks, J. J. (1977). Levels of processing versus transfer appropriate processing. *Journal of Verbal Learning and Verbal Behavior, 16*(5), 519–533.

31 Paivio, A., Walsh, M., & Bons, T. (1994). Concreteness effects on memory: When and why? *Journal of Experimental Psychology: Learning, Memory, and Cognition, 20*(5), 1196.

32 Gick, M. L., & Holyoak, K. J. (1983). Schema induction and analogical transfer. *Cognitive Psychology, 15*(1), 1–38.

33 Carpenter, S. K., & DeLosh, E. L. (2005). Application of the testing and spacing effects to name learning. *Applied Cognitive Psychology: Official Journal of the Society for Applied Research in Memory and Cognition, 19*(5), 619–636.

34 https://www.valamis.com/hub/personalized-learning

35 McEwen, T. (1997), Communication training in corporate settings: Lessons and opportunities for the academe. *American Journal of Business, 12*(1), 49–58.

36 https://whatfix.com/blog/spaced-learning/

6 | Talent Exits

Figure 6.1 iStock.com/simplehappyart
Source: https://www.istockphoto.com/faq/using-files#illustrations-and-vectors

Talent exits present a significant yet often underestimated challenge within the employee lifecycle, marking the phase in which individuals transition out of an organization. This critical juncture can disrupt operational continuity, erode institutional knowledge, and unsettle the very fabric of organizational culture if not navigated carefully. At the heart of effective talent management lies the nuanced understanding and strategic

DOI: 10.4324/9781032711591-6

handling of these departures, ensuring the organization not only remains resilient in the face of change but also thrives.

Recent research underscores the substantial costs associated with employee turnover, which can range from 25% to a staggering 500% of an employee's annual salary, averaging an estimated $13,996 per exiting employee. These figures highlight not just the direct financial implications, but also the indirect costs borne from lost productivity and the adverse impact on team dynamics. The complexity of managing talent exits, therefore, demands a strategic approach to mitigate these financial burdens and preserve the organization's operational integrity.[1]

As we traverse the ever-evolving landscape of talent management, we embark on a journey that transcends the conventional boundaries of human resources. This odyssey guides us through a realm where the departure of talent is not merely a transactional event but a pivotal chapter in the organization's ongoing saga. Here, talent exits are imbued with the weight of myth, where the strategies and processes surrounding talent management transform into epic tales of transition, reflection, and renewal.

In this mystical realm, we encounter enchanted constructs and legendary phenomena that serve as allegories for the challenges and opportunities that talent exits present. These vivid metaphors illuminate the complexities of navigating departures, offering insight and foresight into the art of managing transitions with grace and strategic acumen. As we prepare to unveil these mythical narratives, let us remember that within every tale lies a kernel of truth—a lesson to be learned, a perspective to be gained. These fictional examples, although conjured from the realm of imagination, are deeply rooted in the realities of organizational life, reflecting the universal truths of change, loss, and transformation. So, let us step forward into this enchanted landscape, ready to discover the mythical entities and enigmatic forces that shape the very essence of talent exits:

The Bridge of Farewells: The Bridge of Farewells, a majestic structure spanning the turbulent waters of change, embodies the critical moment of an employee's departure. As individuals cross this bridge, they carry the heavy burden of unspoken words and unresolved feelings, often stemming from inadequate exit procedures or a lack of closure. The challenge arises when the bridge, meant to symbolize a respectful transition, becomes a path of uncertainty due to poorly managed exits. This instability can lead to departing employees feeling undervalued or discontented, tarnishing their final impression of the organization. The real test is ensuring the bridge not only stands firm but also honors the journey of each employee, transforming them into lifelong ambassadors rather than disenchanted leavers.

The Archive of Echoes: Within the hallowed halls of the Archive of Echoes, the whispers of past wisdom risk being silenced forever. This mystical library, a repository of institutional knowledge, faces the daunting task of capturing the essence of departing talent. The challenge here is not just the loss of information but also the fading of nuanced understanding and unrecorded innovations. When employees leave without a systematic knowledge transfer, critical insights vanish into the ether, leaving gaps that hinder the organization's growth and adaptability. Curating these echoes requires more than just documentation; it demands a culture of continuous learning and sharing, where knowledge preservation becomes a collective responsibility.

The Garden of Reconnections: The Garden of Reconnections, with its lush foliage, symbolizes the overlooked opportunity of nurturing long-term relationships with former employees. The challenge emerges when these connections are allowed to wither, untended and forgotten. Organizations often fail to recognize the value of their alumni, missing out on the benefits of mentorship, business opportunities, and enhanced reputation. Cultivating this garden means actively engaging with departed talents, recognizing their ongoing contributions, and creating a vibrant community that enriches both the organization and its alumni.

The Loom of Legacies: At the heart of the Loom of Legacies lies the intricate task of integrating departing employees' contributions into the organizational fabric. The challenge is twofold: honoring their legacy while ensuring the continuity of culture and values. As individuals leave, they take with them unique insights and experiences that, if not captured, can result in a cultural and knowledge vacuum. The loom represents the complex process of storytelling, where each thread—the achievements, lessons, and memories—must be carefully woven to celebrate past contributions while inspiring future generations.

The Portal of Possibilities: The Portal of Possibilities stands as a beacon for departing employees, offering a vision of what lies beyond the organizational boundaries. The challenge here is overcoming the perception of exits as endings, transforming them into opportunities for growth and new beginnings. Organizations often struggle to support transitions in a way that empowers employees to step through the portal with confidence and optimism. Encouraging a positive view of departures requires a shift in perspective, where exits are celebrated as milestones of development and success, not just loss.

The Cauldron of Transformation: Nestled in a mystical grove, the Cauldron of Transformation bubbles with the potential for organizational evolution in response to talent exits. The challenge lies in blending myriad ingredients—lessons learned, skills transferred, relationships forged—into a concoction that fortifies the organization. Stirring this cauldron is an ongoing endeavor, requiring deliberate effort to integrate the diverse elements left in the wake of departures. The true test is in ensuring that the organization not only adapts but thrives on the alchemy of change, emerging stronger and more cohesive.

The mythical landscapes and challenges presented through the fictional concepts of talent exits can be effectively categorized into two overarching themes: 1) operational continuity and knowledge preservation and 2) alumni and network development. These themes embody the core strategies required to navigate the complexities of talent management, especially in the context of departures. By exploring these categories further, we integrate learning science principles to offer innovative solutions and foster a more resilient organizational framework.

Operational Continuity and Knowledge Preservation

Maintaining operational continuity and preserving institutional knowledge during talent exits is a multifaceted challenge that goes beyond simply filling vacant roles. It involves ensuring that critical information and expertise are transferred seamlessly, minimizing disruptions to productivity and organizational effectiveness. Despite the recognition of its

Figure 6.2 iStock.com/champpixs

Source: https://www.istockphoto.com/faq/using-files#illustrations-and-vectors

importance, there exists a significant gap between acknowledgment and action in addressing this challenge.

Research indicates that knowledge transfer is crucial for organizational success, with 75% of professionals considering it important.[2] However, a study by Deloitte's Global Human Capital Trends reveals that only 9% of organizations feel adequately prepared to address knowledge management.[3] This discrepancy underscores the pressing need for organizations to prioritize knowledge preservation during talent exits. Without effective knowledge transfer processes in place, organizations risk losing valuable insights and experiences, hindering their ability to maintain operational excellence and adapt to changing circumstances.

Another critical aspect of operational continuity is succession planning. Effective succession planning ensures that key roles are filled promptly and seamlessly when employees depart. However, only 14% of organizations believe they have an excellent succession plan in place, according to a survey by Deloitte.[4] This lack of preparedness can lead to disruptions in organizational functions and increased risk during talent exits.

To address these challenges, organizations can leverage learning science principles to enhance operational continuity and knowledge preservation. Learning science provides insights into how individuals acquire, retain, and apply knowledge, offering valuable tools for designing effective knowledge transfer processes and succession planning strategies. By integrating learning science principles such as storytelling into knowledge transfer processes, organizations can facilitate the transfer of tacit knowledge and experiences from departing employees to their successors.

Moreover, learning science emphasizes the importance of continuous learning and adaptive thinking, skills essential for navigating organizational transitions effectively. By fostering a culture of continuous learning and innovation, organizations can ensure that institutional knowledge remains relevant and up-to-date, even amid talent exits.

In essence, integrating learning science into operational continuity and knowledge preservation strategies offers a systematic and data-driven approach to addressing the challenges of talent exits. By leveraging learning science principles, organizations can minimize disruptions, preserve institutional knowledge, and maintain operational excellence, ensuring continued success in an ever-changing business environment.

The Science Behind Operational Continuity and Knowledge Preservation

In navigating the challenges of talent exits, organizations must draw on the principles of learning science to ensure operational continuity and preserve critical knowledge assets. Traditional approaches often overlook the dynamic nature of knowledge transfer and fail to address the complexities inherent in employee departures. However, by embracing learning science principles, organizations can develop more effective strategies to mitigate knowledge gaps and maintain operational stability.

Transfer of Knowledge/Skills

In other chapters, we've discussed the concept of transfer of knowledge and how it is notoriously difficult to learn information in one setting and use it in another.[5] This topic again has relevance for knowledge preservation. As individuals prepare to leave an organization, they carry with them considerable knowledge and skills that need to be picked up and used by their successor. Unfortunately, one of the more common means of communicating this information is through written word (if at all!). This means that the successor must transfer organizational knowledge from a document to day-to-day operations—a task that is notoriously difficult. Transfer of knowledge and skills will be enhanced if the learning matches the practice.[6] That is, if we want the successor to be able to best learn and apply the practices of the individual leaving, an apprenticeship model where the successor is doing the work under the supervision of the individual leaving would be ideal for learning.

The Curse of Knowledge and Elaborative Feedback

Experts don't just know more about a topic, they also think qualitatively differently about that information due to the way they organize their knowledge.[7] This reorganization can sometimes make it difficult for experts to recognize how to explain a concept to a novice. This concept is known as the curse of knowledge, a cognitive bias wherein experts have difficulty understanding how novices think.[8] Because of this bias, it is critical that any kind of communication from someone leaving an organization not be one sided. If left up to the relative expert (at least in their role), they will likely suffer the curse of knowledge and ineffectively communicate the necessary knowledge and skills needed for their position. Instead, a receiver of that information should be able to ask quality how and why questions to gain a deeper understanding of the information they are being given. This process is called *elaborative interrogation* and it will allow the learner to better retain and therefore use the new knowledge.[9]

Storytelling

While it is certainly important to convey information as part of knowledge preservation, the manner in which information is shared matters, too. Storytelling is part of human history. It is the way our ancestors passed down information from generation to generation. Because of this, humans are naturally better able to process, understand, and remember information when told it in a story.[10] In fact, when telling a story, the same neural pathways used by the speaker are activated in the listener.[11] Therefore encouraging employees to engage in storytelling about their roles and experiences with an organization will likely aid in the preservation of that knowledge.

By incorporating these learning science principles into their talent exit strategies, organizations can enhance operational continuity, preserve critical knowledge assets, and minimize disruptions caused by employee departures. This proactive approach not only safeguards organizational stability but also fosters a culture of continuous learning and adaptability, positioning the organization for long-term success and resilience.

Applying Operational Continuity and Knowledge Preservation

Navigating talent exits requires a strategic approach informed by learning science principles to effectively mitigate knowledge loss and maintain operational continuity. By leveraging these principles, organizations can develop targeted strategies tailored to the unique challenges posed by talent departures.

Transfer of Knowledge/Skills Example: Implementing structured knowledge-sharing processes tailored to the needs of departing employees is essential for preserving critical institutional knowledge.

Solution: Organizations can adopt similar personalized knowledge transfer mechanisms by implementing mentorship programs, exit interviews, and documentation repositories customized to the departing employee's role and expertise. Boeing's multifaceted approach, including the use of an internal wiki for capturing and sharing knowledge across its workforce, showcases the effectiveness of tailoring knowledge transfer processes to individual preferences. By doing so, organizations can maximize the retention and transfer of critical knowledge assets, minimizing disruptions caused by talent exits. Boeing's strategies highlight the importance of placing relationships and the connection of people above all, ensuring knowledge is not only preserved but also actively shared and utilized across the organization.[11]

Another area in which to use transfer of knowledge and skills is through adaptive succession planning. By identifying potential successors early, based on their competencies, experiences, and developmental needs, organizations can provide them with the necessary practice and preparation. This competency-based approach, aligned with organizational goals, facilitates a seamless transition of knowledge and skills, safeguarding against the disruptions that talent exits might cause. Such strategic planning underscores the importance of readiness and adaptability, preparing the workforce to tackle future challenges effectively.

Traditional succession planning methods, while effective in stable environments, may not suffice in the dynamic and often unpredictable market conditions of the modern world. As such, adaptive succession planning emerges as a vital strategy, emphasizing flexibility, ongoing development, and alignment with changing organizational goals. Adaptive succession planning goes beyond merely identifying potential leaders; it involves a comprehensive approach that prepares the organization for various future scenarios, ensuring continuity and preserving institutional knowledge. By focusing on a competency-based framework, companies can identify and develop potential successors through their skills, experiences, and development needs, aligning these plans with organizational goals for proactive talent gap management and smooth knowledge transition. This strategic alignment is crucial for safeguarding against disruptions caused by unexpected talent exits, ensuring the organization remains resilient and adaptable, ready to face future challenges with a well-prepared workforce.

For instance, organizations aiming to enhance their resilience in the face of market volatility can adopt a model similar to the technology sector's approach to adaptive succession planning. These companies often establish leadership development programs that are deeply integrated with their strategic objectives, focusing on identifying and grooming a diverse pool of talent across various levels. They use a mix of real-world project assignments, cross-functional team collaborations, and formal training sessions to evaluate and develop potential leaders' competencies, experiences, and adaptability.

One practical example could involve a multinational corporation creating a "Leadership Lab" program, where high-potential employees are rotated through different departments and global offices. This exposure allows them to gain a broad spectrum of skills and experiences, while also being tasked with solving real and simulated business challenges. By aligning this hands-on development with the company's strategic goals, the organization ensures a continuous and flexible pipeline of leaders who are not only familiar with the company's core operations but are also prepared to take on leadership roles as the market and organizational needs evolve. This proactive and adaptive approach to succession planning allows companies to better manage talent gaps and smooth knowledge transitions, safeguarding against disruptions and ensuring a resilient and adaptable future leadership.

McDonald's faced significant leadership challenges in the early 2000s, with the sudden loss of two CEOs in less than a year. The company's resilience during this period can be attributed to its effective succession planning strategy. McDonald's had developed a deep leadership bench 6 years prior to these events, preparing multiple internal candidates for potential leadership roles. This approach enabled McDonald's to navigate the crises successfully, with James Skinner stepping up as CEO to continue the turnaround strategy initiated by his predecessors. Skinner's leadership saw McDonald's reach new heights of profitability and market growth. This case exemplifies the importance of having a well-developed succession plan that includes grooming multiple candidates for leadership roles, thereby ensuring organizational resilience and continuity.[12]

The Curse of Knowledge and Elaborative Feedback Example: Cultivating a supportive atmosphere that enables comfortable feedback exchange mitigates the "Curse of Knowledge," ensuring institutional knowledge preservation and fostering continuous improvement. This approach enhances meaningful interactions among employees, reinforcing a culture deeply aligned with the company's core values.

Solution: The Curse of Knowledge illustrates the cognitive gap that can occur when experts attempt to convey complex information to novices, a challenge that Zappos confronts head-on. For instance, when new employees join Zappos, they are not just bombarded with information in a one-sided manner. Instead, they are immersed in a culture of real-time feedback and peer reviews. This method encourages ongoing dialogue, allowing novices to ask critical "how" and "why" questions. An example of this is Zappos' use of interactive onboarding sessions, where new hires are encouraged to question processes and decisions openly, facilitating a deeper understanding through the lens of elaborative interrogation.[13] Zappos' shift from traditional annual performance reviews to continuous feedback loops exemplifies their proactive approach to mitigating the Curse of Knowledge. Employees regularly engage in feedback sessions, where they can receive and give feedback on the spot. This practice was highlighted when a team working on a new website feature presented its progress in a weekly meeting for immediate peer review. The feedback received was not just surface-level praise or criticism but included detailed inquiries and suggestions, fostering a rich understanding and collaborative improvement.

Moreover, Zappos has implemented a mentorship program that pairs less experienced employees with seasoned mentors. This program is designed to bridge knowledge gaps through elaborative feedback.[14] For example, a mentor might use a recent project their mentee worked on as a case study, guiding them through a reflective analysis. This process helps the mentee to not only understand what was done but also why certain decisions were made and how different approaches could lead to varied outcomes, embodying the essence of elaborative interrogation.

Zappos also encourages a holistic view of performance management, integrating personal and professional development. An instance of this is their goal-setting workshops, where employees are encouraged to set both personal and professional goals, with organizational support to achieve them. This approach underscores the importance of individual growth as a component of overall organizational success, fostering a culture where learning is intertwined with daily operations.[14] Incorporating these practices fosters a vibrant, learning-oriented, and high-performing culture at Zappos. Their commitment to continuous feedback, open communication, and a supportive learning environment effectively addresses the challenges posed by the Curse of Knowledge, ensuring that knowledge is not just transmitted but understood and applied. Through these real-world examples, Zappos demonstrates how organizations can create an engaged, motivated workforce capable of navigating complex information landscapes together.

Storytelling Example: Incorporating learning science principles such as cognitive apprenticeships and storytelling into knowledge transfer processes enhances the sharing of tacit knowledge.

Solution: Departing employees create video diaries and interactive tutorials, sharing their insights, challenges, and solutions encountered during their tenure. For instance, consider a scenario where departing employees at a technology firm create video diaries and interactive tutorials. In these videos, they share not only their technical insights but also the challenges they faced and the innovative solutions they developed during their time with the company. This method transforms abstract concepts into tangible examples that embody the company's core values and demonstrate real-world applications. To facilitate this, the organization develops a digital platform that enables the creation, sharing, and integration of these digital stories into its onboarding and continuous learning initiatives. This approach not only captures their invaluable experiential knowledge but also engages and inspires future employees by showing real-world applications of abstract concepts and the company's core values. Organizations can adopt this strategy by developing a platform that supports the creation and dissemination of digital stories and tutorials, integrating them into their onboarding and continuous learning programs. By encouraging outgoing employees to share their stories and lessons learned, companies can create a rich repository of knowledge that is easily accessible. This method not only preserves critical knowledge but also fosters a culture of learning and mentorship, ensuring that the organization's collective wisdom continues to grow and evolve, even as the workforce changes.

Narativ, a pioneer in leveraging storytelling for knowledge transfer, showcases the effectiveness of this approach. By encouraging employees to narrate their experiences, Narativ highlights how storytelling can serve as a powerful tool for preserving and disseminating knowledge, especially in the context of significant labor market changes like the "Great Resignation."[15] This strategy not only ensures the retention of critical organizational knowledge but also enriches the learning experience for new hires, promoting a seamless transition and continuity in the face of workforce evolution. Through such storytelling, companies can build a vibrant culture of learning and mentorship, where the collective wisdom of the organization is continuously cultivated and shared, paving the way for future success.

Alumni and Network Development

The strategic management of talent exits and the effective cultivation of alumni networks are pivotal practices in today's dynamic corporate landscape, essential for fostering organizational resilience, continuity, and innovation. The integration of community-building principles and social learning theories into alumni engagement strategies addresses the challenge of underutilized alumni networks, transforming potential organizational setbacks into opportunities for growth and sustained success.

The criticality of this issue is underscored by networking's cornerstone role in career advancement, with 70–80% of jobs found through

Figure 6.3 iStock.com/Barks_japan
Source: https://www.istockphoto.com/faq/using-files#illustrations-and-vectors

networking, according to the U.S. Bureau of Labor Statistics. This statistic not only highlights the intrinsic value of an active alumni network but also underscores the missed opportunities many organizations face due to engagement shortfalls.[16]

The tangible benefits of a well-engaged alumni network are manifold. For instance, companies such as Tesla, YouTube, and LinkedIn, which owe their origins to the alumni of PayPal, demonstrate the unparalleled potential of these networks for innovation and business development.[17] Additionally, a study by Harvard Business School highlights the financial advantages of strong alumni networks, showing that fund managers connected through educational networks not only placed larger bets on companies within their network but also realized superior performance, with returns nearing 8% annually.[17] Furthermore, the positive impact of alumni networks extends beyond financial metrics to encompass enhanced employer branding, access to a diverse pool of talent and insights, and the stimulation of continuous improvement and innovation. Specifically, their role as a recruitment goldmine and a platform for career advancement and mentorship underscores their critical organizational resource status.

By strategically focusing on alumni and network development and integrating learning science principles, organizations can adeptly navigate the complexities of talent exits. This approach ensures the maintenance of a positive employer brand and leverages the rich experiences and insights that alumni bring to the table, converting challenges into opportunities for organizational strengthening and sustained success.

Viewing talent exits not as losses but as opportunities for enrichment, knowledge transfer, and network building unlocks benefits that bolster organizational resilience, innovation, and growth. Through this lens, talent exits evolve into a continuous cycle of learning, adaptation, and innovation, nurturing an environment in which both the organization and its people can thrive amid transitions.

The Science Behind Alumni and Network Development

Understanding the profound impact of alumni networks on organizational growth and talent management requires delving into the learning science principles that underpin effective alumni engagement. By exploring these principles, we can better comprehend how they foster meaningful connections and contribute to the organization's resilience, particularly in the context of talent exits.

Diversity of Thought

We first discussed the important benefits of a diverse workforce in Chapter 3. But the opportunity of connecting with alumni and maintaining the network of diverse employees only enriches the concepts that we discussed in talent acquisition. A diverse network of alumni creates opportunities for more diverse applicants. In addition, as alumni gain additional experience, networking allows the opportunity for rich ideas to filter back to the organization, creating more creativity and innovation.[18]

Spaced Review

In learning science, spaced repetition/review is one of the most robust strategies for learning and retention.[19] When individuals learn something new, most of that information is forgotten very rapidly, and then the rate of forgetting slows down from there such that a small percentage of the information sticks for a long time. This is traditionally known as the *forgetting curve*. Spaced repetition not only reintroduces individuals to the material, restarting the forgetting curve, it also slows the rate of forgetting.[20] In terms

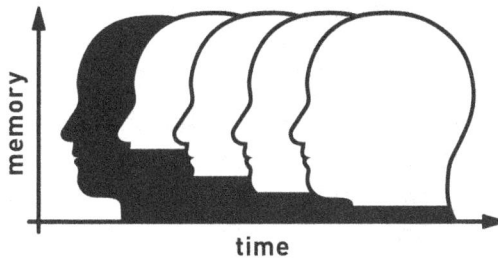

Figure 6.4 iStock.com/sirup

Source: https://www.istockphoto.com/faq/using-files#illustrations-and-vectors

of alumni connections, occasional networking events or messaging helps to keep the organization top of mind when it comes time to make recommendations, connections, or direct possible new applicants.

Social Learning

Another potential benefit to alumni connections involves social learning. One of the principles of social learning theory is that individuals more readily learn and adopt the behaviors of individuals to whom they can relate or whom they admire.[21] Many individuals leave an organization to move on to bigger and better opportunities. If current employees are aware of their connection and have an opportunity to network with former employees, there could be an opportunity for continuous learning and knowledge sharing, as well as motivation to strive for success. Engaging alumni allows current employees to learn from the experiences of former employees, turning talent exits into opportunities for organizational learning and growth.

Integrating these learning science principles into alumni engagement strategies offers a systematic approach to leveraging the latent potential within talent exits. By fostering a culture of continuous learning and collaboration, organizations can transform the departure of employees into a strategic advantage. This not only aids in maintaining a strong employer brand but also ensures that the organization remains resilient and innovative, capable of navigating the complexities of the modern business environment. Through a deeper understanding of these principles, organizations can cultivate alumni networks that contribute significantly to their ongoing success and stability.

Applying Alumni and Network Development

Diversity of Thought Example: Addressing the challenge of maintaining a competitive edge in dynamic industries, leveraging diversity of thought through connections with a diverse alumni network emerges as a strategic solution. As highlighted in Chapter 3, a diverse workforce brings substantial benefits. Extending this to include alumni enriches talent acquisition and reintroduces varied perspectives into the organization, addressing the problem of stagnant innovation and facilitating a culture rich in creativity and adaptability.

Solution: The principle of diversity of thought is integral to driving innovation, fostering adaptability, and maintaining a competitive edge, particularly in dynamic industry landscapes. By integrating this principle with strategic alumni network engagement, organizations can tap into a wealth of diverse perspectives, experiences, and innovative ideas that are crucial for navigating today's complex market environments. Spotify's commitment to diversity and inclusion within its current workforce, exemplified by initiatives such as the Echo and Greenhouse learning portal and the Business Driven Action Learning (BDAL) program, serves as an inspiring model for how these concepts can be extended to alumni networks to further enhance organizational growth and innovation.[22] Spotify's approach, which encourages diverse groups of employees to collaborate, learn from one another, and apply collective wisdom in alignment with business objectives, highlights the untapped potential within alumni networks.[22]

By fostering an inclusive culture that values the varied perspectives of its community, organizations can create a dynamic and innovative environment. This is particularly relevant when considering the strategic engagement of alumni networks. For example, alumni spotlight sessions can be a platform where former employees share new technologies, industry insights, or leadership lessons learned post-departure, injecting fresh and diverse perspectives back into the organization. Similarly, developing mentorship programs that pair current employees with alumni from different backgrounds and industries can broaden the organization's under-standing and approach to problem-solving. For instance, devel-oping mentorship programs that connect current employees with alumni from various backgrounds and industries can significantly expand the organization's problem-solving repertoire. Consider a scenario where a tech startup pairs junior developers with alumni who have transitioned into different sectors, such as fintech or health tech. This cross-pollination of ideas not only enhances the developers' skills but also fosters a broader understanding of how technology can solve complex issues in different industries, strengthening the alumni bond with their former employer and enriching the company culture with a diverse array of thoughts and approaches. These programs not only facilitate the transfer of diverse knowledge and skills but also strengthen the alumni ongo-ing connection with the organization, enriching the company cul-ture with a diversity of thought.

Moreover, inviting alumni to participate in collaborative proj-ects or think tanks can bring innovative ideas and solutions to the forefront, showcasing the value of varied experiences and view-points. Furthermore, inviting alumni to participate in collaborative projects or think tanks can yield groundbreaking solutions. Imagine an annual "Innovation Summit" where alumni and current employ-ees team up to tackle pressing challenges facing the organization. These summits could lead to the development of new products, strategies, or processes that drive the company forward, illustrating the value of integrating varied experiences and viewpoints into the organization's fabric. Such collaborative efforts not only contribute to achieving immediate organizational goals but also underscore a commitment to lifelong learning, development, and inclusivity. These collaborative efforts not only contribute to the organization's immediate goals but also demonstrate a long-term commitment to learning, development, and inclusivity.

Lastly, mirroring Spotify's approach to personalized development through initiatives such as its Talent Snapshot performance review system offers a roadmap for leveraging alumni networks.[23] Initiatives could include hosting alumni development workshops that offer continuous learning opportunities, inviting alumni to participate in innovation projects or hackathons to inject fresh ideas and perspectives, and expanding mentorship programs to include alumni, thereby facilitating a valuable exchange of diverse insights and experiences. For example, an alumni with expertise in blockchain technology could lead a session on its applications and impact on the business, offering a blend of learning and development opportunities that keep the organization at the cutting edge. Additionally, involving alumni in innovation projects or hackathons as mentors or judges can inject fresh perspectives into the organization. A hackathon focused on sustainability, guided by alumni who have pioneered green initiatives in their new roles, can inspire sustainable practices within the organization, showcasing the alumni ongoing contribution to the company's success and reinforcing a sense of community and belonging.

Such efforts not only enhance the organization's innovative capacity but also strengthen the sense of community and belonging among alumni, reinforcing their ongoing connection and contribution to the organization's success. Engaging alumni in such meaningful ways not only leverages their diverse insights for organizational benefit but also reinforces the alumni sense of belonging and value to their former employer, fostering a vibrant, engaged community. This strategy underscores the organization's dedication to diversity, continuous learning, and adaptability, positioning it as a forward-thinking leader in its industry. Through the strategic integration of diversity of thought with alumni network engagement, modeled after Spotify's successful initiatives, organizations can unlock new avenues for innovation, enhance their adaptability to change, and strengthen their competitive advantage in an ever-evolving business landscape.

Spaced Review Example: Addressing the challenge of talent exits, applying spaced repetition strategies revitalizes the exit interview process, transforming it into a dynamic tool for knowledge retention and alumni engagement. This innovative approach ensures a seamless transition of insights, bolstering organizational learning and continuous growth.

Solution: The challenge of effectively managing the talent exit cycle, particularly in preserving institutional knowledge and maintaining engagement with departing employees, is a nuanced problem many organizations face. This issue stems from the natural tendency of individuals to forget information over time, which can be mitigated by applying the principle of spaced repetition/review.

For instance, organizations can tackle this problem by implementing structured exit interviews and knowledge transfer sessions that are followed by periodic engagements with the departing employees. This could take the form of alumni newsletters, regular networking events, or even short, targeted training sessions designed to refresh their knowledge of company practices and innovations. Such engagements not only help in keeping the organization top of mind for alumni but also encourage them to remain active in the company's network, potentially facilitating rehires or referrals.

The traditional approach to exit interviews often reduces them to a mere checklist item, a procedural step that fails to capture the depth of knowledge and insights departing employees can offer. This reductionist view represents a missed opportunity for organizations to deeply understand the reasons behind employee turnover, gather constructive feedback, and identify areas for improvement. Instead of being a valuable tool for organizational learning and development, exit interviews have become a formality that rarely leads to actionable insights or meaningful change.

Addressing this problem requires a reimagining of exit interviews as a strategic component of the talent exit cycle. For instance, organizations can transform exit interviews into comprehensive knowledge transfer sessions. These sessions would not only delve into the reasons for departure but also focus on capturing the departing employee's unique insights, experiences, and suggestions for the future. By treating these interviews as crucial learning moments, companies can uncover patterns that might indicate systemic issues, gather suggestions for improvement, and identify opportunities to enhance the workplace culture.

Incorporating innovative exit interview practices can significantly improve how organizations manage talent exits, capture invaluable insights, and maintain engagement with departing employees. A standout example in this space is Parkview Health, which partnered with Work Institute to understand the specific causes of first-year nurse turnover. Through detailed exit interviews, Parkview Health was able to implement several strategic interventions, such as building out a nursing career ladder and revamping the orientation and onboarding process, which resulted in a 34% reduction in first-year turnover across the included departments.[24]

This case highlights the importance of moving beyond traditional exit interviews, often seen as mere formalities, to a more strategic and comprehensive approach. By treating exit interviews as key learning opportunities and incorporating spaced repetition through follow-up engagements, organizations can uncover deeper insights and actionable feedback. This approach not only addresses the immediate challenges but also contributes to long-term strategic planning and organizational development.

Moreover, understanding the common barriers to effective exit interview participation is crucial. For instance, ensuring confidentiality and offering various formats for exit interviews, such as online surveys or third-party interviews, can increase participation rates and the quality of feedback received. By addressing concerns over potential consequences and time constraints, and clearly communicating the mutual benefits of the exit interview process, organizations can foster a more open and honest dialogue with departing employees.

Furthermore, incorporating elements of spaced repetition could rejuvenate the value of exit interviews. Following the initial exit interview, organizations could schedule follow-up conversations or surveys at regular intervals, such as after 3 and 6 months. These follow-ups can provide additional perspectives on the employee's experiences and insights after they have had time to reflect on their tenure. This spaced approach not only keeps the dialogue open but also allows for the collection of more nuanced feedback that can inform long-term strategic planning and organizational development. By reevaluating and innovating the exit interview process, organizations can turn a routine procedure into a strategic asset, enhancing their understanding of workplace dynamics and improving retention and engagement strategies.

In addition, leveraging technology platforms that enable former employees to access training materials and updates about the company at regular intervals can also serve as a practical solution. This approach ensures that the knowledge and connection to the organization are not only maintained but also strengthened over time, despite the physical departure from the company. By addressing the problem of exit interviews head-on and embracing spaced repetition strategies, organizations can not only improve the process of talent exit but also ensure that the knowledge, insights, and networks of departing employees continue to enrich the organization.

This approach transforms the end of an employee's tenure into the beginning of a valuable, ongoing relationship that benefits both the individual and the organization, fostering a culture of continuous learning, innovation, and mutual growth.

Social Learning Theory Example: Social learning theory emphasizes learning through social interactions and observations within communities. It highlights how individuals can gain knowledge and behaviors by observing others, particularly in collaborative environments.

Solution: To enhance talent management and leverage social learning theory, organizations can create engaging alumni networks. This strategy involves fostering a global community where former and current employees exchange insights, which benefits both parties and strengthens organizational knowledge. By doing so, companies can turn talent exits into opportunities for continuous learning and development, maximizing the collective expertise within their networks. Accenture's Alumni Network demonstrates the practical application of social learning theory by fostering a global community for knowledge sharing and networking among former employees. This approach capitalizes on the theory's emphasis on learning through social interaction, allowing the organization and its alumni to mutually benefit from continuous engagement and exchange of insights. Accenture's strategy highlights the value of maintaining strong connections with alumni, thereby enhancing organizational learning and development opportunities.[25]

To leverage social learning theory in enhancing talent management, organizations can undertake several practical steps. For instance, they could develop structured mentorship programs that pair former employees with current ones, facilitating the exchange of knowledge and experiences. This not only strengthens the alumni network but also enriches the organizational learning environment.

Additionally, companies can organize regular knowledge-sharing webinars or workshops led by alumni, covering topics relevant to both the organization's current projects and broader industry trends. These sessions offer an interactive platform for current employees to learn from the vast experiences of their predecessors, promoting a culture of continuous learning and development.

Furthermore, creating online forums or digital communities where current and former employees can interact, ask questions, and share advice can also be highly effective. These platforms allow for ongoing engagement and make it easier for knowledge to circulate within the organization, leveraging the collective expertise of its network to solve problems and innovate.

By adopting these strategies, organizations can transform talent exits into opportunities for continuous learning and development, maximizing the collective expertise within their networks and fostering a global community for knowledge sharing and networking.

Conclusion: Embracing the Future of Talent Lifecycle

The comprehensive exploration of talent exits, integrating the insights from learning science and strategic HR practices, culminates in recognizing the multifaceted approach required to navigate this critical aspect of talent management effectively. As organizations grapple with the challenges of talent exits, from preserving institutional knowledge to maintaining engagement with departing employees, adopting innovative strategies becomes paramount.

Operational Continuity and Knowledge Preservation

The necessity for a structured approach to knowledge transfer is evident in the example of structured exit interviews and knowledge transfer sessions, followed by periodic engagements such as alumni newsletters and networking events. These strategies underscore the importance of leveraging spaced repetition to counteract the forgetting curve, ensuring that the organization remains a focal point for alumni, potentially facilitating rehires or referrals.

Redefining Exit Interviews

Addressing the shortcomings of traditional exit interviews requires transforming them into comprehensive knowledge transfer sessions, as highlighted by the success story of Parkview Health, which partnered with Work Institute.[26] Through detailed exit interviews and strategic interventions, Parkview Health was able to significantly reduce first-year turnover, showcasing the benefits of a strategic and comprehensive approach to exit interviews.

Incorporating Technology

Leveraging technology platforms for former employees to access training materials and updates ensures that knowledge and connection to the organization are maintained and strengthened over time, in spite of physical departures. This approach emphasizes the value of spaced repetition strategies and the role of technology in enhancing the talent exit process.

The Importance of Diversity of Thought and Social Learning

Spotify's initiatives, such as the Echo and Greenhouse learning portal, exemplify the significant advantages of fostering diversity of thought to spur innovation and learning. Likewise, Accenture's Alumni Network showcases the effective application of social learning theory, highlighting the pivotal role of alumni engagement in promoting mutual growth and facilitating the exchange of knowledge. These examples underscore the critical importance of integrating diverse perspectives and collaborative learning frameworks within and beyond the organization to drive continuous development and innovation.

As organizations look ahead, the evolving dynamics of the workforce, with the introduction of new generations, necessitate a vigilant and adaptive approach to talent management. Embracing diversity and inclusion, leveraging technology for strategic advantage, and prioritizing employee well-being and development will be crucial. In this transformative era, talent management becomes not only a strategic imperative but also a cornerstone of organizational longevity, inviting a journey of innovation, empowerment, and evolution. This journey ensures that as employees exit, new possibilities and opportunities continually arise, perpetuating a legacy of success and resilience in the ever-changing business landscape.

References

1   https://sajhrm.co.za/index.php/sajhrm/article/view/873
2   https://www.shrm.org/topics-tools/news/hr-magazine/capture-what-employees-know-before-they-leave-the-company
3   https://www2.deloitte.com/xe/en/insights/focus/technology-and-the-future-of-work//organizational-knowledge-management.html
4   https://action.deloitte.com/insight/1874/how-to-put-the-success-in-succession
5   Gick, M. L., & Holyoak, K. J. (1980). Analogical problem solving. *Cognitive Psychology, 12*(3), 306–355.
6   Morris, C. D., Bransford, J. D., & Franks, J. J. (1977). Levels of processing versus transfer appropriate processing. *Journal of Verbal Learning and Verbal Behavior, 16*(5), 519–533.
7   Chase, W. G., & Simon, H. A. (1973). Perception in chess. *Cognitive Psychology, 4*(1), 55–81.
8   Camerer, C., Loewenstein, G., & Weber, M. (1989). The curse of knowledge in economic settings: An experimental analysis. *Journal of Political Economy, 97*(5), 1232–1254.
9   Pressley, M., Symons, S., McDaniel, M. A., Snyder, B. L., & Turnure, J. E. (1988). Elaborative interrogation facilitates acquisition of confusing facts. *Journal of Educational Psychology, 80*(3), 268.
10 Landrum, R. E., Brakke, K., & McCarthy, M. A. (2019). The pedagogical power of storytelling. *Scholarship of Teaching and Learning in Psychology, 5*(3), 247.
11 https://usaidlearninglab.org/community/blog/why-boeing-focused-behaviors-not-tools-when-building-its-km-strategy
12 https://www.sigmaassessmentsystems.com/mcdonalds-succession-case-study/
13 https://www.zavvy.io/hr-examples/employee-performance-reviews-at-zappos
14 https://www.fearlessculture.design/blog-posts/zappos-culture-design-canvas
15 https://narativ.com/employee-onboarding/knowledge-transfer-storytelling/
16 https://jobs.washingtonpost.com/article/how-to-land-a-job-by-networking
17 https://enterprisealumni.com/blog/the-power-of-corporate-alumni-networks
18 Wang, J., Cheng, G. H. L., Chen, T., & Leung, K. (2019). Team creativity/innovation in culturally diverse teams: A meta-analysis. *Journal of Organizational Behavior, 40*(6), 693–708.
19 Weinstein, Y., & Sumeracki, M. A., (2019). *Understanding how we learn: A visual guide (O. Caviglioli, Illus.).* David Fulton, Routledge.
20 Ebbinghaus, H. (1885/1964). *Memory: A contribution to experimental psychology.* Dover Publications.

21 Marx, D. M., & Ko, S. J. (2012). Superstars "like" me: The effect of role model similarity on performance under threat. *European Journal of Social Psychology, 42*(7), 807–812.

22 https://www.zavvy.io/hr-examples/employee-development-at-spotify

23 https://www.zavvy.io/hr-examples/employee-performance-reviews-at-spotify

24 https://workinstitute.com/engagement-retention-services/exit-interviews/

25 https://www.accenture.com/us-en/careers/explore-careers/area-of-interest/alumni-careers

26 https://workinstitute.com/engagement-retention-services/exit-interviews/

7 Cycle Begins

Figure 7.1 iStock.com/cagkansayin

Source: https://www.istockphoto.com/faq/using-files#illustrations-and-vectors

As we reach the culmination of our exploration into the talent cycle within organizations, we reflect on the stages we've journeyed through: talent acquisition, management, retention, and exits. Each phase, with its unique challenges, underscores the need for innovative solutions. Enter learning science—a dynamic and powerful tool that promises to revolutionize how we approach these challenges. For each chapter, we are including some high-level takeaways as a quick reminder of the chapter content and applications.

DOI: 10.4324/9781032711591-7

While we may be at the end of this book, we hope that you are just at the beginning of your journey. And while learning about learning science is one part of that journey, we don't want it to end there. In the pages that follow, we encourage you to take the same evidence-informed strategy described here in all aspects of your work. Seek out research to support your practices and the ones that are encouraged by others. And know that no one strategy will work in all situations with all people. It is imperative that you collect your own data to determine when and how your changes are effective.

Learning Science in Talent Acquisition

Talent acquisition in a broad category. It includes everything from a needs assessment at the organization, job descriptions, advertising, application portals, selection, interviewing, hiring, and onboarding. Additionally, there is consideration of salary expectations and benefits packages.

We chose to focus on just two distinct categories of talent acquisition where learning science can support your work.

Strategic Talent Sourcing

We started our exploration of talent acquisition with strategic talent sourcing. How can we get the right candidates to ultimately apply and stay interested throughout the process? The first step is to consider candidate motivation. To move candidates from a job ad to an application, they need to feel confident in their ability to be successful. Applications full of jargon or complicated systems are less likely to be filled out. Applicants also need to stay engaged and therefore touchpoints with those applicants will improve the chances of an eventual hire. But you only want to hire those candidates who are a good fit for the role. Making sure that candidates understand the culture of the organization through the use of dual coding and concrete examples will help the applicants see how the values of the company play out in everyday activities.

Ideally, you will have a diverse candidate pool to stimulate creativity and innovation in your organization, but you must be mindful and have a concrete strategy to mitigate possible implicit bias in your hiring procedures. Finally, we discussed the importance of building up a positive company reputation through the use of feedforward strategies for candidates who are not selected. They may be more likely to reapply for other roles and to encourage others to apply when they are given clear, actionable feedback about how to improve moving forward.

Optimized Onboarding

A great deal of learning takes place during onboarding and that learning can happen in such a way that it sticks, or is easily forgotten. Our recommendations for onboarding are to differentiate new hires such that those with more expertise receive different training than those who are relative novices. The training itself should be spaced out in time so that new employees get reminders about the material and also so that they don't get depleted trying to learn everything in a short time. New employees need practice when learning new knowledge or skills. They should be given many opportunities to apply what they are being taught so that they better understand it and retain it. Throughout their onboarding, new employees need lots of actionable feedback so that they can more quickly learn from mistakes, again making the practice opportunities critical in the onboarding process.

Who is doing the training matters quite a bit as well. By utilizing a mentorship model, new employees are provided with psychological safety, personalized learning, and opportunities for feedback from someone who is "in the trenches." They also have an opportunity to learn from observation, further enhancing the learning process.

Learning Science in Talent Management

Talent management is an umbrella term that truly can encompass everything in this book (hence, the title), but in this section of the book, we focused primarily on how to optimize the productivity of your team once they have been hired. While talent management could certainly involve a focus on the individual—how to get them to do more work or how to make sure the right person is in the right role—we take a broader view and look at the team. How can we make sure that, collectively, our employees are doing their best work?

Leadership Development and Career Pathing

To maximize the potential of future leaders for our teams, leadership development must be a priority. But not all leadership development is created equal—neither should it be! Individuals enter leadership development at different stages of their career and their understanding of leadership should be considered. Differentiated programming is recommended. Within that programming, individuals should learn about self-awareness to maximize their potential so that they can continuously learn and grow even after formal programming. They should be given opportunities to practice new skills and feedback throughout the process. Feedback should also come from all levels so that developing leaders have the opportunity to hear from employers, peers, and direct reports. Building a feedforward culture that encourages everyone to give and receive feedback has a huge impact on growth and achievement.

Organizational Culture and Employee Well-being

That feedforward culture will only be successful in a culture that encourages psychological safety. Managers need to be equally vulnerable in receiving feedback from others and create a system of trust where employees do not need to be fearful of the outcomes of taking chances. A natural byproduct of a feedforward culture is enhanced emotional intelligence and a recognition that we can all develop skills over time if we maintain a growth mindset. While psychological safety impacts employee well-being, there are other needs that should be considered. In particular, employees need to feel as though they have some choice and control over their environment, they need to feel competent to do the work they are asked to do, and they need to feel like they are not alone in that work. Making sure that these needs are met will improve employee well-being, job satisfaction, and ultimately organizational outcomes.

Learning Science in Talent Retention

Talent retention is closely related to talent management. In both cases, we are in the middle part of employment, and creating an effective team clearly impacts talent retention. But here we are focused on keeping good talent. While in management, we were focused on fostering a positive work environment, here, we turn to the individuals themselves and how to keep them loyal and engaged so that we avoid quiet or active quitting.

Employee Engagement

Employee engagement is fundamentally about motivating employees to want to do their work. They need to understand how this work is valuable to them as individuals and the choices they have in the way in which they complete the work. They need to feel confident that they will be successful, which can be achieved by breaking large projects into manageable chunks. When they do succeed, they need recognition for their accomplishments. Recognition can be as simple as a shout-out in a weekly meeting or more substantial like a bonus on a paycheck, but knowing that hard work is noticed and appreciated encourages more hard work. Recognition doesn't have to come from a manager, however; encouraging relationships between peers can make employees feel as though they are not alone in their work.

Learning and Development

If employees view their positions as "dead-end jobs," they are likely to put far less effort into the work and may spend work hours looking for other positions. Fostering a culture of learning and development is key to helping employees see the value in their employment. In addition to retaining talent, learning and development have the potential to enhance the existing team and create future leaders for the organization. As we saw in the other chapters, learning should be differentiated for employee needs and prior knowledge. Individuals will vary in their interests and future goals and these must be considered when creating L&D options. Within L&D programming, employees should have plenty of opportunities to immediately practice the new skills they are developing and to return to any newly acquired knowledge over time. In this way, no training will ever be "one and done," but strategic reminders and practice with the material will guarantee that it was not a waste of time, money, or energy.

Learning Science in Talent Exits

All good things must come to an end. In our chapter on talent exits, our goal is to ensure that when talented individuals leave an organization, there is a smooth transition. We are not so much focused on the operational challenges of exit interviews and conflicts of interest. While those topics are important, learning science more readily informs how to preserve the institutional knowledge of our employees and the benefits of remaining connected to them after their departure.

Operational Continuity and Knowledge Preservation

Often when an individual leaves an organization, the person stepping into that position is experiencing the work for the first time. A more effective way of creating operational continuity is to allow for a certain amount of overlap through thoughtful succession planning or mentorship models. The goal is to allow the employee to step in time to practice the skills they are being taught under the watchful eye of the individual departing. If this is not possible, it's important to note that the individual leaving will likely suffer from cognitive biases, limiting the amount of information they consider critical to pass down. This can be mitigated through an elaborative feedback session where they are asked questions about any information they have shared and through storytelling, where the individual leaving can share background and contextual information which may be critical for institutional knowledge preservation. Storytelling can also be used more broadly throughout an organization to provide important context to otherwise bland messaging.

Alumni and Network Development

For the vast majority of organizations, once an employee leaves, the relationship ends. Here we encourage companies to consider maintaining an alumni network where former employees receive communications from the organization, but also where the organization utilizes the connections and knowledge from their network. There are many positive outcomes from maintaining an alumni network, many of which we discussed in other areas of the book. More diverse experiences mean more creative ideas, so harnessing alumni experiences could promote innovation, especially as current employees look to alumni as potential role models for inspiration. In addition, alumni know the inner workings of the organization and the type of candidates who might be best for a position. By maintaining communications, your organization can stay top of mind for alumni who have the potential to send qualified future employees your way.

Evidence-based Decision Making

This book is not comprehensive when it comes to talent management or when it comes to learning science. There is so much more to learn. But as you develop new ideas and research ways to improve your organization, we hope that you will consider the approach that we have taken here. At the end of each chapter, we have a list of references, many of them academic publications to support the ideas we have developed. The learning science concepts in this book have robust research to support their use in many different contexts (or we wouldn't have included them).

As you develop new ideas, take the time to make sure that the methods you are considering have science to support their use. Just because it is common practice, does not necessarily mean that it is an *effective* practice. Take, for example, the very common practice of assessing and catering to learning styles. The learning styles hypothesis is that we each have unique learning needs. I might be a visual learner and you might be an auditory learner therefore we need different types of training to succeed. This extremely popular idea has no research to support it.[1] In fact, the research that has attempted to "prove" this theory has shown that individuals can learn in lots of different ways; they just have preferences for how they would like to learn.[2] Because of this, the learning styles hypothesis might actually be causing harm.[3] By labeling someone as an auditory learner, they might then believe that they are not going to learn much from visual information and vice versa. Because of the relationship between self-efficacy and motivation, individuals might check out before they even start trying to learn.

Learning styles aside, our goal is to encourage you to be skeptical and thoughtful about the approaches used in your organization. When possible, seek out research to support your practices, and do not solely rely on anecdotal evidence that someone tried it and liked it. Rather, do a little digging about the pros and cons of a given strategy and the outcomes of practice before implementing them. For those things you are already doing, perhaps consider a self-audit where you examine those strategies to determine what is evidence-based and what is not.

Evaluating Changes

We hope that you will walk away from this book inspired and intrigued to make changes in your organization. But there are a *lot* of strategies in this book and not all of them are likely to be good fits for your organizational needs. Our recommendation is not to change everything at once, but rather to make small meaningful changes to your strategies that will have meaningful impacts.

As good practice, however, you need to have a plan for data collection and analysis before you make any changes. You need to be able to determine if your changes are having the impact that you want them to. While it is important to research a change before implementation, it's also important to do your own research, collect your own data, and make sure the change is worthwhile.

Consider the following example. Let's say that your current onboarding could use some work. Right now, employees listen to various members of the organization telling them the most important things they need to know before they can start working. This takes two 8-hour days and the employees then spend the next 3 days shadowing someone in their department before they start work. There are some good things here but certainly some improvements to be made. Let's say you've just finished reading Chapter 3 on talent acquisition and you want to add spaced retrieval to your onboarding. Before you start, you need to ask yourself, "How do I know that employees aren't remembering as much as they should?" What data can you collect that demonstrates that this is an issue? Ideally, after you implement spaced retrieval, you would be able to look at that same data for the new group of employees and see improvement. If you don't, then either the intervention needs to be tweaked or possibly scratched. Either way, you wouldn't know if you were wasting resources unless you have the data to indicate whether your efforts made a difference.

We hope that you will consider lots of changes after reading this book, but we also hope that you will implement those changes carefully and with a plan to measure their impact.

Call to Action

As we draw our exploration to a close, it's evident that learning science transcends being a mere toolkit; it is a foundational aspect of modern talent management. This interdisciplinary field, melding insights from psychology, neuroscience, and pedagogy, has the transformative potential to revolutionize each segment of the talent cycle. Its principles and methodologies offer more effective, efficient, and engaging solutions that can significantly enhance organizational success and employee fulfillment.

The integration of learning science within the talent cycle isn't just about adopting new techniques or tools; it's about a paradigm shift in how we understand, engage, and develop our workforce. By applying the lens of learning science, organizations can navigate the complexities of talent acquisition, management, retention, and exits with greater ease and effectiveness.

To the leaders, HR professionals, and all those dedicated to nurturing talent within their organizations, we extend a heartfelt invitation: embrace the power of learning science in your talent management strategies. Begin by segmenting your talent cycle and evaluating each part through the lens of learning science. This comprehensive review will not only help you identify areas of improvement but also provide a roadmap to address these challenges more effectively.

Seek out resources that can deepen your understanding of learning science and its application in the workplace. Engage with experts who can offer insights and guidance on how to integrate these principles into your organizational practices. Be open to innovation, and don't shy away from experimenting with new approaches and strategies, but be sure to have a plan for measuring their effectiveness.

171

Remember, the journey toward a more effective talent cycle, guided by the insights of learning science, is not a solitary endeavor. It requires a collective commitment to change, a willingness to embrace new possibilities, and a shared vision of creating a workplace where every individual has the opportunity to grow, contribute, and thrive.

Your commitment to this journey can lead to a workplace that not only excels in managing talent but also fosters a culture of continuous learning, innovation, and employee engagement. The future of talent management is bright, and it's within your power to shape it. Let's embark on this transformative journey together, one step at a time.

References

1 Pashler, H., McDaniel, M., Rohrer, D., & Bjork, R. (2008). Learning styles: Concepts and evidence. *Psychological Science in the Public Interest, 9*(3), 105–119.
2 Massa, L. J., & Mayer, R. E. (2006). Testing the ATI hypothesis: Should multimedia instruction accommodate verbalizer-visualizer cognitive style? *Learning and Individual Differences, 16*(4), 321–335.
3 Sun, X., Norton, O., & Nancekivell, S. E. (2023). Beware the myth: Learning styles affect parents', children's, and teachers' thinking about children's academic potential. *Science of Learning, 8*(1), 46.

Index

For Product Safety Concerns and Information please contact our EU
representative GPSR@taylorandfrancis.com
Taylor & Francis Verlag GmbH, Kaufingerstraße 24, 80331 München, Germany

www.ingramcontent.com/pod-product-compliance
Lightning Source LLC
Chambersburg PA
CBHW050655280326
41932CB00015B/2920